NEW ENGLISH FICTION

MW01705872

Playing the Game

THE PITCH
Rebecca Adlard

FRUIT COCKTAIL
Frank Brennan

THE CLEOPATRA CLUB
Antoinette Moses

ELI

P.O. Box 6 - Recanati - Italy
Tel. +39/071/75 07 01 - Fax +39/071/97 78 51
E-mail: info@elionline.com - www.elionline.com

Editor
Maria Cleary

Series editors
Antoinette Moses
Alan Pulverness

Illustrations
Andrea Goroni

Printed in Italy - Tecnostampa Recanati 03.83.186.0

ISBN 88 - 536 - 0040 - 3

Contents

Preface 4

The Pitch
About the Author 6

The Pitch
Before Reading 9

The Pitch 10

The Pitch
After Reading 36

Fruit Cocktail
About the Author 44

Fruit Cocktail
Before Reading 47

Fruit Cocktail 48

Fruit Cocktail
After Reading 71

The Cleopatra Club
About the Author 80

The Cleopatra Club
Before Reading 83

The Cleopatra Club 84

The Cleopatra Club
After Reading 109

Preface

This volume of new English fiction contains three stories which are all about games. The word is used in its widest sense. Not only games as in sports or forms of entertainment but also the games people play in society in order to get what they want.

The first story, *The Pitch*, takes the reader into the future. The story is set behind the scenes in a television company, where an ambitious young producer is trying to sell his new game show to a group of cynical executives. They think have seen it all before until they are drawn into The Hunt. A frightening look at how far reality shows might go in the search for audiences.

The second story, *Fruit Cocktail*, is a comedy about a weightlifter who is determined to win the world championship. The story is told by one of the competitors, whose coach has very strong ideas about his diet. The story is quite humorous, yet it also deals with the serious problem of performance-enhancing drugs in sport.

The third story, *The Cleopatra Club*, is also about the desire to win. Caroline Kitson wants to win the game of life. The story is set in a college at the University of Cambridge, where an ambitious student sets up a club for career-oriented female students. To join the club, the young women have to prove themselves in some rather unusual ways. Unfortunately, things go wrong when one student takes a dangerous risk.

Rebecca Adlard

The Pitch

About the Author

Rebecca Adlard has combined teaching English with a drama career for the past ten years, working throughout the world as a teacher and teacher trainer. She has scripted plays in conjunction with the Bedlam Theatre Company in Cornwall and is currently collaborating with Lingua-Arts in Madrid on a version of *Othello*, as well as writing a one-hour play, *Extras*, and co-authoring *Richmond Adventures*, a series of interactive story books for young learners.

Ask the Author

Was there anything you read or watched on television that gave you the idea for this story?

I remember when I was quite little, watching a programme which showed clips from television from around the world. One of the host's favourites was a Japanese game show, 'Endurance'. During one clip contestants were put into completely enclosed glass compartments on a beach under the hot midday sun. The heat must have been unbearable. To make the 'game' even tougher, huge blocks of ice were left to melt on the beach just outside each glass compartment. The winner was, of course, the last contestant to give up. At the time I thought that it was very odd, to want so desperately to be the winner that you would undergo such torture; now it seems that this kind of show is becoming increasingly popular. With programmes such as 'Big Brother' and 'Survivor', it appears that people are willing to do almost anything for prizes or their fifteen minutes of fame.

While writing *The Pitch*, I read several newspaper articles about reality TV, especially about some bizarre new American game shows which combine quiz shows with endurance tests. It seems that anything quirky or strange can be made into a prime-time network hit. *The Pitch* is about taking reality TV to its limits, while we ask ourselves: how far will things go?

Have you ever pitched for anything yourself? If you have, what was the experience like?

I have pitched in writing but never in a face-to-face presentation like in the story. I think it must be terrifying to have to try to convince people in a very limited time that you have a great idea while facing rejection of something that may have taken you months or even years to develop. I wanted Guy and Linda to show this sense of desperation as well as conveying the cold and inhuman aspect of a pitch and the judgmental world we live in. Maybe this is a clue to understanding Guy and Linda's seemingly inhuman behaviour. They have been treated badly, judged harshly and been made to feel inferior, and so in turn, they view their 'contestants' in the same way.

The story has some of the qualities of an action film. When you write a story, do you imagine it as a film?

Oh yes, most definitely. As I have a background in drama and the theatre, spectacle is very important to me. I also have an over-vivid imagination; as I'm typing, my fingers can hardly keep up with the images that flash through my mind. In *The Pitch* it was important for me to convey the idea that the executives and Internet viewers are watching a live show. I also wanted the 'game' to have the elements of an action movie, as I believe that contemporary audiences, especially younger viewers, have lost the ability to be entertained with clever wordplay, and look for thrills and stimulation. Programme makers constantly have to come up with new ways of entertaining their audiences. Viewers have become anaesthetised to the most extreme scenes of murder, war and mutilation. If a film or a TV programme doesn't scare, excite or thrill them in every scene, it seems they lose their concentration and turn to something else. Just think of the special effects that are needed in films nowadays just to hold viewers' attention. Writing the story as if it was a film, I hoped I, too, could excite, thrill and hold the attention of my readers.

Do you feel the events described in the story could really happen one day, or is it just fantasy?

I think it is happening already, to some extent. Just consider the physical danger that some game shows inflict on their contestants. Producers of some American game shows subject contestants to extreme temperature changes and mild electric shocks while they answer general knowledge questions. More seriously, a recent British radio show asked contestants to sit on blocks of ice to win tickets. As a result several people suffered extreme ice burns and were in hospital for weeks, and some have been scarred for life. It seems only a matter of time before somebody dies taking part in one of these games.

Prisoners take part in reality talk shows in the US and I recently read a proposal for a programme where a 'fugitive' is let loose across America and the audience have to help track him or her down. Whether society will ever allow real prisoners to be used as contestants remains to be seen, but I have to say that for me there is a frightening logic in the premise of *The Pitch*, which with the wrong people in power, could quite easily turn this story into reality!

Before Reading

Ⓐ The word 'pitch' can mean:

- a sports field ☐
- voice quality ☐
- a sales presentation ☐
- the location of a market stall ☐
- the slope of a roof ☐

What do you think it will mean in this story?
Do you think it will have more than one meaning?

Ⓑ Now read the first paragraph of the story and say why you think the author has chosen to use this title.

Ⓒ The story is about a 'reality' television show. Read the titles and descriptions of some current or recent British TV programmes below. Which ones are reality shows?

- 'The Trench' – relive the First World War ☐
- 'Who Wants to be a Millionaire?' – win a million pounds! ☐
- 'Survivor' – who will survive on the island and win a million pounds? ☐
- 'Castaway' – how will they survive on a lonely Scottish island? ☐
- 'Big Brother' – who will be last in the Big Brother? ☐
- 'Wheel of Fortune' – turn the wheel and win the money! ☐

Ⓓ Match the following words with their definitions.

pilot	way of getting away from reality
fantasy	person who chooses to do something
interactive	first show of a TV series
escapism	when information is exchanged
contestants	imagined, not real
volunteer	people who take part
executives	number of people watching a show
ratings	people who make decisions

The Pitch

The atmosphere in the room was tense. Guy flicked* his eyes from side to side, trying to catch a glimpse* of the executives'* faces. He'd been here before*; the trick* was not to let them know that he wanted to see their expressions. He saw Linda's red hair bounce* slightly and knew that she was doing the same. She knew the business as well as he did, and she had as much interest in this as he had. They'd invested* everything in this project*: their money and the last two years of their lives. Everything they had was tied up* in it: their dreams, their hearts and their souls*. If these execs didn't like it, if they didn't buy it, then Guy and Linda would be out of the game* for good.

Guy felt sick to the very pit* of his stomach. He tried to swallow, but he couldn't. He tried to ignore his nerves and launched in*.

"So, what does audience research* show us? People are becoming more sophisticated and demanding* in the programmes that they want to watch. They can't be fooled* by inferior* shows. They want something different."

"We know that, but what exactly do you think they want?" asked the youngest of the three execs. He was about twenty-eight, Guy thought, obviously a high-flyer*. He was very confident, dressed from head to toe in black. Black boots, black jeans, black polo neck, black mobile in

flicked: moved quickly
glimpse: quick look
executives (execs): people who make decisions and are in control
been here before: done this kind of thing before
trick: skill
bounce: move up and down
invested: put
project: (here) television show
tied up: put (and can't be touched)
their hearts and their souls: every part of them
the game: the television business
pit: bottom
launched in: began his speech
audience research: results from asking audiences what they want
demanding: difficult to please
fooled: deceived
inferior: less good
high flyer: someone who does well early in their career

his trendy* black thigh pocket, and even a black designer goatee* on his narrow chin. The only things that Guy could find that weren't black were his eyes, which were green. Bright, green, suspicious* eyes, like a cat's. Guy found that he often identified* people with animals. It made them easier to sell to. And that was what he was here to do. Sell.

Guy took a deep breath.

"They want a new show. They want a show that makes them feel empowered*. And, at the same time, they want to believe that there is a different reality out there somewhere. A reality that is more exciting, more alive than their own."

"In other words, you're saying they want fantasy, escapism*," came the comment. This cat was going to give Guy a run for his money*; Guy could feel it.

"Well, yes and no," Guy replied carefully. "The key is to create a fantasy world that reflects the audience's own world. It has to feel real. Audiences don't want shows that are simply escapist – they want reality. That's why they'll love 'The Hunt'. 'The Hunt' will give them reality. It won't be staged*; it will be exciting, tense, competitive and interactive. Everything that audiences want."

"So, how is it unique*?" a quiet, even* tone from the only female exec.

Guy had decided that she was a deer. She wore a simple, elegant trouser

trendy: fashionable
goatee: small beard forming a triangle in the middle of the chin
suspicious: not trusting
identified: matched
empowered: given power
escapism: way of escaping from reality
give . . . a run for his money: make him work hard
staged: false; artificial
unique: different from anything else
even: flat, level

suit in grey. She looked smart and ordered* and contained*. She had a thin, delicate face with a very cute* nose and watchful* eyes. He felt that he had to be careful with her; she might be difficult.

"OK. This is what 'The Hunt' is about: a team of ten people are sent to an island. Abandoned*. They need to learn the skills of survival*. So what we've got here," Guy felt more confident now, "is the sociological* aspect* of group dynamics*, the psychological aspect of people being stripped of normality* and having to adapt*. Then there is the gaming element*: they've got a task to carry out. There are ten items* hidden around the island. The team will have one week to find the items using location maps. The game is pacey*, exciting."

No comments yet. That was good; they were interested. Now it was time to produce the first ace from his pack*.

"However, we're not going to let our audience feel left out or distanced* from the game, merely shouting advice at the screen. No. In 'The Hunt', the audience are part of the game, too. They can log on to our website, pick and choose which camera they want to view through, and then send information that will affect the state of play* on the island. For example, they can send messages to the hunters. Yes, there's a team of hunters trying to stop the contestants and they'll have access

ordered: organised and regular
contained: with self-control
cute: pretty; attractive
watchful: guarded and suspicious
abandoned: left on their own
survival: how to live in difficult conditions
sociological: relating to society
aspect: part
group dynamics: how a group behaves and works together
stripped of normality: with all normal life taken away
adapt: change behaviour in different situations
gaming element: game part of the show
items: things
pacey: fast
the first ace from his pack: (here) the first argument that will convince them
distanced: kept at a distance from
state of play: how the game continues

to pick-up points* throughout the island. Naturally we won't interfere* with any of the messages. So the audience could be sending true or false information to the hunters. The hunters won't know. To sum up: in 'The Hunt' you have ten hunters trying to find ten contestants* who are trying to find ten items. If they find them all, the game stops and the surviving contestants win their freedom."

"Freedom?" echoed the deer.

"What happens when one of these hunters finds a contestant?" It was the suspicious tone of the cat again.

"When a hunter is successful in finding and stopping a contestant, then the team is down to nine. And the remaining contestants must find all the items before the hunters find them," Guy said smoothly.

He knew he mustn't tell them too much too soon; he had to hook* them first.

"Haven't we seen all this before?" asked the cat. "People left to survive and form relationships with strangers that they don't really like, in strange environments. We've seen search-and-find game shows, shows that test mental and physical skills, on sets designed to look like Atlantis or the ancient Aztec world. We've seen weird* game show hosts, we've seen tough guy presenters*, we've seen them helping, we've seen them hindering*, we've seen them comforting and we've seen them laughing at and deriding* contestants. This isn't anything different, it's too

pick-up-points: places where they can receive messages
interfere: stop or change
contestants: those taking part in a game
hook: catch their interest
weird: strange, odd
tough guy presenters: people who present shows pretending to be hard and unkind to contestants
hindering: making it harder
deriding: making fun of

contrived*, audiences are bored by reality TV now. It's nothing new."

Not such a suspicious tone now, more aggression* creeping in*. Guy felt a moment of panic*; he was losing them. He told himself to keep cool.

"Except that in this game, in 'The Hunt', there isn't a presenter. No host. I promise you, it's not like any previous show. The island isn't a set* and these are not ordinary contestants."

"What do you mean, 'not ordinary'?" the deer responded quickly.

"I mean, our contestants are not from Joe Public*," Guy began.

"Then where are they from?" interrupted the cat.

"From Suanzista. They are all volunteers* from Suanzista."

"Suanzista?" echoed the deer. "You mean they're all prisoners?"

"Yes," Guy replied. He'd got their interest now. "And what's more, they're all prisoners on Death Row*. The Hunt offers them a choice, they can either remain on Death Row and who knows, maybe their appeals* will come through* at the eleventh hour*, or they can sign up* to play the game and take their chances on the island. If they make it*,

contrived: unrealistic
aggression: anger
creeping in: gradually becoming noticeable
panic: extreme fear
set: place where TV shows are made
Joe Public: ordinary people
volunteers: people who freely choose to do something
Death Row: where murderers are kept before they are executed
appeals: requests to save their lives
come through: be received
eleventh hour: at the last minute (before something happens)
sign up: agree formally
make it: are successful

then I have an agreement from Suanzista that by taking part in 'The Hunt', the prisoners will have repaid* their debt to society* and will be free men and women once more."

There was a silence in the room; Guy steadied his breath* for the final part of the pitch.

"What we are offering you is real, it's the next step in home entertainment. Can you afford not to sign this up?"

"Hmm...maybe," replied the cat. Sweat made Guy's brow tingle*.

"Look," Guy spoke urgently*. "Other reality television shows offer danger, too, but it's fake* danger and the audience knows that. These are angry times, people need to get rid of their anger through what they experience in the media if not they go out and vent their frustrations* in the streets, on each other. These contestants are terrorists, political activists*, or as some people see them, freedom fighters. They've already shown that they are willing to fight and, if necessary, die for what they believe in. What's more, this is going to be like a public debate. Everybody has an opinion about these people, about capital punishment*, about prisoners' rights*. By choosing whether they help the contestants or the hunters, people will be able to make their opinions known. It's as if they're being allowed to vote. They will feel as if they are being listened to, that what they do makes a difference.

repaid: paid back
debt to society: what they owed the world (for their crimes)
steadied his breath: made himself breathe regularly
made Guy's brow tingle: Guy felt the sweat on his forehead
urgently: quickly; with feeling
fake: false; untrue
vent their frustrations: violently express their feelings of anger and helplessness
political activists: people who work on behalf of a political party or from strong political beliefs
capital punishment: punishment by death
prisoners' rights: what prisoners should get, or be allowed to do

The show can't lose: the prisoners get a chance for freedom, the public get a real sense of the danger and at the same time they have their say. In addition, the authorities have fewer inmates* in their prisons, they pay for fewer executions* and society gets rid of all its frustrations." Guy paused for breath. "And we, or rather you, get a top money-spinner* that will knock everything else off the ratings*. Now, you tell me where you've seen that before."

That was it. There was nothing else he could say. They had to bite* now or it was all over.

"Do you have anything we can see?" It was the first time that this exec had spoken. When Guy had first seen him, he'd felt his presence* – this was a powerful man – and he was somewhat* surprised by the gravelly* Northern accent. "Have you got a dossier* or anything like that?" he asked Guy.

It had taken quite a lot of time for Guy to think of the right creature for this third exec, but now he had no doubt. He was an owl. It scared him slightly when he came across a 'bird'. He didn't like the otherness* of birds; their ability to fly, the beat* of their wings. If you looked into a bird's eyes, you could never work out what they were thinking. And so, you could never anticipate* their reaction. The owl was older than the other two execs. His hair was turning grey at the temples*. There would be no pulling the wool over his eyes*. But now, Guy allowed himself a little smile.

inmates: prisoners
executions: when prisoners are killed
money-spinner: something that makes money
knock everything else off the ratings: be the most successful programme
bite: show their interest
he'd felt his presence: he had been strongly aware of him
somewhat: quite
gravelly: deep
dossier: collection of papers
otherness: the way birds were different
beat: movement made by birds' wings
anticipate: work out in advance
temples: flat areas on the head at the side of the forehead
pulling the wool over his eyes: deceiving him

"Oh yes," he said, turning on his laptop, which was connected to a large screen at the far end of the room. "Better than a dossier, we've got the show live* on the web for you."

"What!" exploded the cat, "How come*?"

"We've been preparing a pilot show for some time. The teams landed on the island two days ago. Perhaps you'd like to see some of the action that we recorded yesterday?"

With slightly stunned* looks on their faces, the execs all swivelled* in their chairs to face* the screen.

"Linda, can you get the lights* please?" Guy felt in control of the situation again. He had at least fifteen minutes while they were watching to evaluate* the best way to present the next stage of his pitch. He logged on and scrolled down* to 'The Hunt'. The computer whirred* and the screen in front of them flickered* and came to life*. Suddenly, they were on a long, sandy beach with a turbulent*, muddy sea crashing onto the shore. There were ten people on the beach, all bent double* scanning* the sand as if they were searching for a lost contact lens. One of the women dropped to her knees and starting running her hand over the sandy surface.

"What are they doing?" came the cat's voice.

live: in real time (as they watch)
how come?: how have you done this?
stunned: amazed
swivelled: turned round
face: turn towards
get the lights: turn off the lights
evaluate: work out
scrolled down: moved down the screen
whirred: sound made by the computer
flickered: quickly came on and off
came to life: started working
turbulent: rough
bent double: bent over towards the ground
scanning: looking carefully

"Searching for one of the ten items," Linda answered evenly. Guy felt very grateful to her.

The woman was now digging furiously* and calling the others over. Her voice was distant and came in waves*.

"Is that as good as the sound quality gets?" This cat was making life difficult. Yet again, cool as a cucumber*, Linda came to the rescue.

"Unfortunately, we're picking them up on camera eight. Camera ten is closer, but . . ."

She leaned across Guy in a fragrant* whirl* of perfume and pressed a couple of keys on the computer. Now they were looking onto a dry track* heading upwards through a canopy* of broad-leafed tropical trees. They could hear the excited voices quite clearly.

"I've got it . . . I've got it!" It was the woman's voice, followed by a man's urgent tone: "Quick, give it to me" and various whoops* of joy.

Linda leaned in again and changed the screen back to the original view. Now they could see a huge man delicately* wiping the sand off a small object. Linda pressed another key and the camera zoomed in on the man's enormous hands. He was holding a bracelet made of blue and green Paua* shell.

"Is that one of the items?" the deer asked. "It's lovely." Linda nodded, "Retrieval* of item number one. Now keep watching."

furiously: very fast and hard
in waves: it came and went several times
cool as a cucumber: very calm
fragrant: sweet smelling
whirl: circular pattern of air
track: path
canopy: covering
whoops: loud cries
delicately: gently
Paua: New Zealand shell
retrieval: finding

Linda began to tap quickly on the keyboard. Then, just like an action movie, the screen started to cut* from one view to another as different cameras picked up different parts of the chase. Images of frightened, desperate* faces came and went amidst* ominous* glimpses of black. The execs could clearly hear gasps* and violent gulps* of air being pulled into aching* lungs*. Then Linda pressed another key and the video screen flickered slightly and went blank*.

The screen had been dead now for five, six, seven, eight seconds. Guy heard a voice in his head counting along with his heartbeat, but not his breathing. He'd been holding his breath now for eight, nine, ten seconds. Still no one spoke. This was taking a long time, what were they thinking?

"That was amazing . . . really, really amazing!"

Guy slowly released* his breath. It was amazing, because it was the cat speaking. Maybe the show was good enough. Maybe his pitch had been good enough. The cat was still talking and he seemed hooked.

"It's exciting. It's really exciting!"

The deer turned her gaze* onto Guy. "It's good." She nodded her head slowly. "What happened next?" she asked softly.

Guy saw Linda turn and smile at the deer. He heard her say lightly,

cut: move from one scene to another when filming
desperate: very frightened
amidst: among
ominous: suggesting something bad is about to happen
gasps: short sounds of breath being taken in
gulps: sound of swallowing
aching: hurting
lungs: organs that control breathing
blank: empty
released: let go of
gaze: long intense look

"Capture* number one."

Now let's hook our feathered friend*, Guy thought. At that he turned to look at the owl and raised his eyebrows as if he was about to ask a question. The owl was sitting with his hands together, fingertips tapping gently, rhythmically against his jaw*.

"Hmm," murmured the owl. Guy found himself holding his breath again. The owl nodded slowly. "Hmmm … I think I'd like to see a bit more."

"Yes!!" thought Guy. "We're in!*"

Twenty minutes later, Guy was feeling quite a bit more relaxed. With coffee cups in front of them, the cat, the deer and the owl looked expectantly* at Guy and Linda. Guy brought up a map of the island onto the screen. The island was about fifteen miles from north to south and twelve miles across. The execs could see a high mountain peak* to the north and gentler* slopes to the south and the east.

"The ten red circles you can see," Guy explained, "are the ten hidden items. The two that are flashing are the items that the team have already found."

"And the team has this map, too?" asked the deer.

"Yes," replied Guy. "The team leader has a map. The only difference is that our map also shows us where each camera is. The hunters don't

capture: act of catching someone
feathered friend: bird (here, the owl)
jaw: lower part of the face
we're in!: we've done it!
expectantly: waiting for something
peak: top of a mountain
gentler: not so steep

have a map at all, they must rely* on luck."

"And audience help," commented the owl. He was talking more now, Guy noticed.

"Exactly," said Guy as he switched the image on the screen.

"Who's that?" asked the deer.

They all looked at the screen in time to see a slim, young girl with short dark hair. They hadn't noticed her before. The girl scrambled* awkwardly over a collapsed* wall and disappeared from view.

"Ah, that's Gina," said Guy, bringing up* Gina's dossier. "On the website there's a fact file and an interview with each contestant, giving their age, background and reason for wanting to play the game."

"Isn't that obvious?" interrupted the cat.

Guy smiled as sweetly as he could and continued. "Let me just play you one part of Gina's interview."

They could see a still* picture of Gina grinning sheepishly*, then the picture came to life and they heard Gina's excited voice saying: "I feel that I've made mistakes in my life, but I think everyone has. This is a turning point* for me, a new opportunity to be the person I'm meant to be. I have a lot of good qualities and I hope to learn from my fellow contestants."

rely: depend, trust
scrambled: moved with difficulty, often using one's hands
collapsed: fallen
bringing up: showing on the screen
still: not moving
sheepishly: looking embarrassed
turning point: time in life when you make a dramatic change

"Why was she in prison?" asked the deer.

"She was a messenger for the SLF, the Stodec Liberation Front," replied Linda.

"Isn't she sweet?" Guy asked, freezing Gina's face, "We think she'll be very good in bonding* the team together. OK, back to the island in real time. Camera nineteen, Linda. Let's see what Gina's doing."

Gina was moving towards a ruined* chapel. It seemed as if the team leader was using her as some kind of decoy*. Looking at their maps, the execs could see that she wasn't moving towards any of the items. Then they read the message that had come through from a viewer:
`GINA'S HEADING AROUND* THE DESERTED* CHAPEL ON HER WAY TO THE NORTH POINT.`

Gina was now moving very slowly, with only low cover*. As the hunter approached, Guy heard the deer's hushed* and hurried "Move, move." But Gina couldn't hear, of course, and she hadn't seen the approaching hunter. There was the sudden sound of gunfire*.

The execs gasped as Gina fell. The conference room felt as if the air had been suddenly sucked out of it*. The camera then zoomed in on* Gina. She was shaking with fear, looking down at the wound* on her leg.

bonding: bringing together
ruined: that had fallen down
decoy: person or animal used to attract hunters towards it (and away from something/someone else)
heading around: moving around
deserted: alone and empty
low cover: with nothing high to hide behind
hushed: quiet
gunfire: sound made by guns
sucked out of it: removed from it
zoomed in on: filmed close-up
wound: injury (here: caused by gunshot)

"Is she OK?" asked the deer in worried tones, looking towards Guy and Linda.

"I guess she's out of the game," said the cat.

"But, for goodness' sake, she's bleeding!" screeched* the deer. "Is there someone to help her? I think she needs help. She looks scared. What happens now? What do we do? How do we get her out?"

Guy did not reply.

"Good grief! Look at the viewing figures!" It was the owl.

Guy looked from the image of Gina on the screen to the viewing figures in a side column*. It showed a dramatic* rise.

"The audience love it," he said. "They feel as if they're gods, giving information as and when* they choose, deciding if a contestant should have a chance or not". I was right, he thought, this is what they want; the power to make a difference, to control someone else's life, because their own lives are so out of control, so controlled by others.

"Shall we take a lunch break?" Linda's clear voice broke the silence as she flicked to camera eight and froze* the picture on the screen, a calming view of the seashore*. "I don't know about anyone else but I'm starving*," she said, smiling at them all.

screeched: shouted in a high tone
side column: list at the side of the screen
dramatic: great and surprising
as and when: whenever
froze: stopped completely
seashore: where the sea meets the land
starving: very hungry

After lunch there was a pervasive* air of well-fed, sleepy contentment* in the conference room. The execs were now watching live coverage of two of the contestants, the team leader, Jed, and Al. For the last forty-five minutes they had been battling* their way uphill against a fast and furious* tropical storm that had been beating down on them. They had now reached a small clearing*, through which water was rushing in a newly-formed* rainwater stream. The rain had virtually* stopped and the two contestants were now searching for the next item.

"So, tell us about these two." The cat said sleepily, as he arched his back in a long stretch.

Guy brought up the fact file on Jed. He was big and broad with a wild look. A beast of a man*. He had an interesting face, very interesting. Was there something reckless* or foolhardy* about it? Somehow Guy and Linda had known immediately that he would be the team leader.

"We knew that without a good leader for the team, the game would soon become boring and predictable*." Guy explained. "We wanted someone special, and I have to say it wasn't easy. We experienced certain psychological difficulties in finding a good leader from the bunch of 'applicants'* that we had to choose from.

pervasive: spreading among all of them
contentment: quiet happiness
battling: fighting
fast and furious: short but with great energy
clearing: space between trees
newly-formed: new
virtually: almost
beast of a man: big animal-like man
reckless: irresponsible
foolhardy: someone who takes unnecessary risks
predictable: the results can be known in advance
'applicants': (ironic) they could not apply freely as they were prisoners

But Jed is an ex-commando* who went off the rails* a bit. Post-war syndrome*. Tried to assassinate* a general he thought had failed his troops*. He didn't succeed, of course, but it means that for our purposes he's highly trained, both physically and mentally."

"Can we hear some of his interview?" asked the deer.

"Of course, but I warn you, he's a man of few words*." Guy answered, clicking on the icon.

On screen they could now hear Guy's disembodied* voice talking over Jed's impassive* face.

"So, why should we give you, and not one of the others, the chance to play the game?" asked Guy.

A slight smile appeared at the left corner of Jed's mouth as he looked straight into the camera and replied, "No reason at all."

"But you do want to play the game?" Guy's voice persisted*.

"Better than being cooped up* in here. I'm a soldier. I'll take my chances out there any day," was the reply.

"What would you say if we asked you to be the captain of the team?" Guy asked.

ex-commando: former member of a special fighting force
went off the rails: behaved crazily
post-war syndrome: a psychological condition affecting soldiers after a war
assassinate: kill
failed his troops: had led his soldiers badly
of few words: who doesn't talk much
disembodied: without a body
impassive: showing no emotion
persisted: continued to ask
cooped up: shut up

Jed gave another smile, slightly broader this time. "Are you asking me?"

Guy continued to probe*. "What if we were?"

"I'd say 'Why not?'" Jed looked straight at the screen. His image froze there.

"I see what you mean," said the cat. "The strong, silent type. Well, he should definitely be macho* enough to get good female ratings." He gave the deer a sly* look. She blushed* slightly and asked, "What about the other one?"

"Ah, Al." said Guy. He fiddled* with the keyboard and Al's face, framed with a mop* of floppy hair*, appeared on the screen. This time Linda's voice floated* into the viewing room.

"So, why do you want to play 'The Hunt'?"

They saw Al rock* slightly in his chair and give a strangled* half-laugh as he said, "Because being away from my wife and my two little boys is killing me*. I'll do anything to get out of here, anything."

"Do you think you can hack it* on the island?"

"I don't know, but you've got to give me the chance, please," Al replied in an anguished* voice.

probe: ask questions
macho: a man who appears strong and brave
sly: secretive
blushed: her face turned red
fiddled: did something
mop: (here) untidy hair
floppy hair: hair that falls on the face
floated: could be heard
rock: move from side to side
strangled: stopped as soon as it starts
killing me: hurting me badly
hack it: (slang) manage the situation
anguished: full of pain

"Do you think that you'll be one of the survivors at the end?" Linda asked him.

Al gave that small laugh again. "I hope so. My boys need a father, and I'm the only one they've got."

"Excellent," murmured the owl.

"He looks so innocent. What did he do?" asked the deer, turning to look at Guy and Linda.

"The authorities took Al's third son away to a clinic because he was born with . . ." Guy paused. "Imperfections*. . . he'd slipped through* the genetic screening*. Al tried to get him back. He broke into the compound* and held one of the doctors hostage* and threatened to kill him."

"Oh!" exclaimed the deer.

"And what about the hunters, do you have interviews with them, too?" the owl asked Guy.

"No," Linda interjected*. "We want to create some mystique* around them. Shall we get back to the action? Several messages have just come through to the hunters, giving away Al and Jed's position. Let's see what happens, it should be good. Uh . . . camera thirteen, I think."

imperfections: things wrong with him
slipped through: escaped attention
screening: test
compound: square area surrounded by fence or wall
held . . . hostage: captured in order to get something
interjected: interrupted
mystique: feeling of mystery

The camera zoomed in on Jed's worried face. He was scanning the vicinity*, glancing* every so often up a tall tree. Camera thirteen showed Al climbing up the tree. He was moving towards a nest which contained a clay pipe*. Just as Al reached out to grasp the thin clay pipe, a shot rang out* from below and two of the hunters could be seen labouring* up the slope. The camera angle changed as Guy flicked to camera fourteen for a close-up of the hunters. It was clear that they hadn't yet seen Jed, but they had a good view of Al perched* in the tree.

The execs saw one of the hunters stop and steady himself* to take aim at Al again. The second shot whistled* past his leg and as Guy switched back to camera thirteen, Al lost his balance. He tried to stop himself from falling by dropping the pipe and grabbing at a branch, but he missed it and fell the five metres to the ground. There was a strangled wail* as he landed on his ankle, which twisted* under his weight. They heard him hiss* through the pain, "Go, Jed, just go! I think I've broken my ankle. Go!"

Then Jed was running, running fast. Guy was having difficulty changing from camera to camera to keep up with him. As he flew* past each camera, they could hear great big gulps of breath. They watched as he crashed* through streams, half running, half sliding* down the mossy* ravine*. He seemed to be taking the most difficult-looking route* in order to shake off the hunter.

vicinity: area around them
glancing: looking quickly
clay pipe: object made from dried earth and used for smoking
rang out: was heard
labouring: moving with difficulty
perched: up in the tree (like a bird)
steady himself: become calm and stand straight
whistled: sound made by the passing bullet
wail: cry of pain
twisted: turned over
hiss: 's' sound of breath leaving the body
flew: ran fast
crashed: moved noisily
sliding: moving fast down a slope, sometimes lying down
mossy: covered with moss, a flat green plant
ravine: deep narrow valley
route: way

"He's really fit*," exclaimed the cat with admiration.

"Ex-commando," Linda gently reminded him.

"He's trying to tire the hunter," joined in the deer excitedly.

They watched as Jed climbed higher and higher, never seeming to tire. The hunter started to fall behind and realising this, Jed made a swift* right turn into thick foliage* and was lost from the sight of the camera. The hunter hadn't seen Jed change direction and flashed past the camera. Several moments later, they watched as Jed reappeared and, like a fox, turned back on his own tracks* and went down the hill away from the hunter. As he passed the camera, they noticed that he was smiling.

"Can we go back to Al?" asked the deer.

Back in the clearing, Al was leaning against a tree and talking to a hunter. "You've got to help me," Al grimaced*. "I've done something to my ankle . . ."

The hunter remained silent. Then he raised his gun and pointed it at Al's chest. With a look of sheer terror* on his face, Al struggled* to sit upright*. He put his hand out in front of him. Back in the conference room Guy felt the hairs on the back of his neck stand up and that horrible sensation of frost* running down his spine*. This was the

fit: strong and healthy
swift: fast; sudden
thick foliage: lots of bushes and trees
tracks: marks made by moving along a path
grimaced: made an expression of pain
sheer terror: extreme fright
struggled: tried very hard
sit upright: sit straight
frost: icy cold
spine: bones down his back

moment that could make or break* it for him. He watched as the hunter stepped forward, took aim and shot Al. The front of Al's jacket turned scarlet* and he slumped* forward into a heap that looked too small to be a person.

"Great capture . . . and it was all based on information from the audience, fantastic," said the cat.

"Now, the members of the audience who supplied* the information which enabled* the hunter to find and destroy the team member will receive free online watching minutes," Linda explained.

"Hold on*," the owl interrupted. "Hold on....What?... No way*!"

"Sorry?" asked Linda.

"Look at the viewing figures; up another nineteen percent," said the owl. "Unbelievable!"

Linda visibly relaxed, "And messages are up thirty-two percent. This is the viewing experience that people have been looking for."

Guy rubbed the back of his neck and allowed himself a small smile and a long breath. "More messages come in with each capture," he told the execs.

"What about Jed?" asked the owl.

make or break: be decisive
scarlet: red
slumped: fell
supplied: gave
enabled: allowed
hold on: stop!
no way: (slang) that's not possible!

"Interestingly, they seem to like Jed," said Linda. "If you look at a selection of the messages," with this she flashed them up on the screen, "you'll see that the ones concerning Jed are all red herrings*."

"But we could change that," said the owl slowly. "We're viewers too, aren't we?"

"Yeah," breathed the cat.

Linda seemed puzzled*, "What do you mean?" she asked.

"They mean that they want to send a message," Guy explained.

The owl's message flashed up onto the screen:
JED IS ON THE NORTHWEST POINT OF THE ISLAND, HE'S MAKING CAMP IN AN OLD DISEASED TREE TRUNK. THE GROUND LOOKS SLIGHTLY SCORCHED* AS IF THERE HAS BEEN A RECENT FIRE!
Immediately what seemed like a thousand other messages started to appear on the screen.

NO, HE'S NOT!

HE'S AT THE OTHER END OF THE ISLAND.

JED'S ON THE BEACH, NEAR THE LANDING PAD*.

"The viewing figures are going through the roof*. Fantastic!" the cat purred*.

red herrings: deliberately false information
puzzled: confused
scorched: burnt
landing pad: place where helicopters land
going through the roof: rising very high
purred: low sound made by a happy cat

“There’s a hunter picking up our message right now,” said Linda switching to camera two.

The hunter clearly wasn’t sure where Jed was. He moved very quietly and slowly. It was pitch dark* now and they were watching the hunter through the eerie* infrared light that each webcam was equipped with*. They were all silent, hardly daring to breathe, straining* to hear Jed make a move. Then they heard it. A slight rustle*, so slight that it could have been a lizard or a bird, just off to the left, by the old gnarled* tree.

“There! Did you hear that?” whispered the cat excitedly.

“Look!” squealed* the deer. Jed’s head had appeared for a split second* from one of the tree trunks. The hunter hadn’t seen him. He was crouching* about five metres away with his back to the trunk, waiting. They waited. Five seconds, six, seven, eight. The tension in the room was palpable*. Then, like a rabid dog*, Jed hurled* himself through the opening in the trunk and landed on top of the hunter. But, the hunter had obviously heard Jed, too, because just as Jed fell on him, he twisted round and Jed was suddenly splayed out* on the ground. They heard the air blast* from his lungs with the full force* of his fall. Guy couldn’t help feeling slightly disappointed that Jed had been psyched out* so easily. He had hoped for more from Jed. And he was the last of the team; this looked like the end of the game. Maybe the execs would think that the game was too short.

pitch dark: completely dark
eerie: strange
equipped with: had
straining: making a great effort
rustle: small noise like leaves moving
gnarled: old and twisted
squealed: said in an excited, high tone
split second: very brief moment
crouching: sitting close to the ground
palpable: could be felt
rabid dog: dog with rabies (hydrophobia)
hurled: threw
splayed out: spread out
blast: exit with force
full force: all the weight
psyched out: (slang) tricked

"Jed's fighting back!" exclaimed the deer.

"I don't believe it," the owl said excitedly. "You're right. Fantastic! Look at those viewing figures! Just think of the money we can make from advertising," he added. "Guy, you said it, this is the real thing."

"Linda, maybe now's the time to get those bottles of bubbly* out of the fridge," Guy said, looking around the room triumphantly*.

Linda moved towards the door, but couldn't quite tear her eyes away* from the screen, where Jed and the hunter were grappling* on the ground. It was difficult to tell who had the advantage*. Then, with no warning, Jed stopped. He staggered* to his feet and stumbled* to a tree. The hunter wasn't moving. With some effort, Jed steadied himself and walked over to the man's side.

bubbly: (slang) champagne
triumphantly: like a winner
tear her eyes away: look away from
grappling: fighting closely together
had the advantage: was doing better than the other
staggered: got to his feet with difficulty
stumbled: walked with weak steps, half falling

Guy switched to camera fifteen. Now they were looking down on the scene. They watched as Jed removed the man's visor and recoiled*. The hunter's brown eyes were wide open and stared at the camera with a glazed* expression. Jerkily, Jed lurched* away from the body and retched* violently. Then he looked directly at the camera.

"Stop this," he yelled. "Stop this … game! He's dead! This is sick! You're sick! Listen to me, he's dead!"

There was absolute silence in the viewing room.

"There's something that bothers* me," the owl said finally.

Guy froze.

"I want to change the name. I want to call it 'It's Your Choice'. Now, where do we sign?"

recoiled: moved back suddenly in horror
glazed: without expression
lurched: moved suddenly
retched: made the sound of being sick
bothers: worries

After Reading

Response

Ⓐ Read the following reactions to the story. Which one is the closest to how you feel? What else could you add?

I'd hate to live in a world like that. ☐
What an amazing game – I'd love to see it! ☐
The way things are going, someone is going to get killed on a reality TV show. ☐
If the pitch is right, you can sell anything. ☐

Ⓑ There are two settings for this story – the conference room and the island. Which one seemed more real to you? Say why.

Ⓒ Which character did you dislike most and why?

Comprehension

Ⓐ Use the following words or phrases from the story to complete the sentences:

- empowered ☐
- high-flyer ☐
- identified ☐
- interest ☐
- invested ☐
- reality ☐

Guy and Linda had an equal .... in the project.
They had .... more than just money in it.
Guy thought people wanted to feel ....
The youngest executive was clearly a ....
Guy found selling easier if he .... people with animals.
Guy thought that audiences wanted to experience a different kind of ....

After Reading

Ⓑ Tick all of the following that correctly describe 'The Hunt'.

- It takes place on an island. ☐
- There are the same number of contestants and hunters. ☐
- There are five prizes to be won. ☐
- At the end of the game the contestants win their freedom. ☐
- The audience follows the action on the Internet. ☐
- The audience can send information to both the contestants and the hunters. ☐

Ⓒ Write down six things you know about the contestants who are taking part in 'The Hunt'.

Ⓓ How do the execs react when Guy tells them that the show has already begun? Give two examples.

Ⓔ "I've got it ... I've got it!" (line 176) Who has got what? Why do they want it and where are they?

Ⓕ Each of the execs react differently to Gina's capture. Match the quotes with each of the three execs. What do you think each one feels about Gina at this moment?

"Is she OK?" ....
"I guess she's out of the game." ....
"Good grief, look at the viewing figures!" ....

Ⓖ Why do you think the contestants need a good leader? Do you feel that Jed is the right person for the job? Why/Why not?

Ⓗ Why was Al in prison?

After Reading

Ⓘ "But we could change that... We're viewers too, aren't we?" What does the owl mean and what does he do?

Ⓙ The owl suggests changing the title of the show from 'The Hunt' to 'It's Your Choice'. Do you think this is a better title? Can you suggest any other title for the show?

Plot and Setting

Ⓐ The story opens with this sentence: 'The atmosphere in the room was tense.' Why do you think the author begins at this point? What is happening and what has happened before the story begins?

Ⓑ At what point in the story do the execs start watching the action on the island? What effect does this have on the plot?

Ⓒ What clues are there in the text to suggest when the story takes place?

Ⓓ The reader sees the events on the island via the screen in the conference room. How would the reader be affected if the story took place on the island? Do you think it would be more or less effective?

Theme

Ⓐ Choose one of the following themes and demonstrate how it fits the story.

- Survival of the fittest ☐
- The dangers of 'reality' TV ☐

- Giving the public what it wants ☐
- Freedom and censorship ☐
- Modern-day gladiators ☐

Ⓑ Where in the story do you think you perceive the author's point of view? What is it?

Ⓒ Why do you think reality TV shows are popular? Would you ever take part in one? Why/Why not?

Narration and Style

Ⓐ 'He knew he mustn't tell them too much too soon; he had to hook them first.' What techniques does the author use to create suspense? In answering this question you may like to think about the following:

- flashbacks ☐
- cuts between locations ☐
- information that is gradually revealed ☐
- use of 'real' time ☐

Can you think of any other techniques?

Ⓑ There are a number of places in the story where the identity of the speaker is not stated. Does this matter? Why/Why not?

Ⓒ What is the effect of using the Internet messages? Describe the style in which they are written.

After Reading

Character

Ⓐ Guy gives each of the three execs an animal identity. Why do you think he chooses a cat, a deer and an owl? Does this help you to see the characters more clearly?

Ⓑ Which characters do you know most about and which least about? Does this affect the way you respond to them?

Ⓒ Match the following adjectives used in the story to the correct characters.

contained	....
suspicious eyes	....
a powerful man	....
watchful eyes	....
short dark hair	....
excited voice	....
a beast of a man	....
innocent	....

Vocabulary work

Ⓐ The words below all describe some kind of movement.

bolted	flew	lurched	staggered
crashed	huddled	scrambled	stampeding
crouching	hurtled	sliding	stumbled
dodging	labouring	slumped	weaving

Which of the words describes:

A fast movement?	....
An unsteady action?	....
An indirect movement?	....
Movement with difficulty?	....
Not moving?	....
Uncontrolled movement?	....

Ⓑ The following list of antonyms is jumbled. Find the correct matches.

fantasy	interested
split up	turbulent
hindering	*reality*
careful	huddled together
unique	foolhardy
bored	helping
calm	ordinary

Ask the Author

Ⓐ Are the following statements True or False?

	True	False
The author has pitched in face-to-face presentations.	☐	☐
The author thinks it must be frightening to spend a long time developing a project.	☐	☐
The author thinks it must be frightening to face the possibility of a project being rejected.	☐	☐
The author thinks the process of pitching excuses the behaviour of Guy and Linda.	☐	☐

After Reading

Ⓑ Which of the following phrases refer to the author and which refer to the viewers?

	Author	Viewers
over-vivid imagination	☐	☐
just want thrills and stimulation	☐	☐
become anaesthetised	☐	☐
lose concentration	☐	☐
could excite, thrill and hold the attention	☐	☐

Ⓒ Which of the following has already happened on TV and radio game shows and competitions and which does the author think could happen in the future?

	Has happened	Could happen
Contestants suffer temperature changes	☐	☐
Contestants suffer electric shocks	☐	☐
People end up in hospital	☐	☐
People die	☐	☐
Prisoners are used as contestants	☐	☐

Follow-up

Speaking

In groups take turns to make a pitch for your favourite TV show.

Writing

Write a dialogue between Guy and Linda after the meeting.

Or

Write a dialogue between the execs about the show, six months later.

Class activity

Stage a class debate: "Reality television goes too far".

FRANK BRENNAN

Fruit Cocktail

About the Author

Frank Brennan is a teacher and writer. He has published two collections of short stories for adult language learners.

Ask the Author

The story has a lot of detail about the sport of weightlifting. Have you ever been a weightlifter, or are you just a fan?

I've never been a weightlifter, though I used to go to the gym years ago. That, however, was just to keep fit – I was not at all like the weightlifters in my story. During that time, I did meet a number of people who were seriously devoted to bodybuilding. I always think people with obsessions of one kind or another are fascinating, and I had them in mind when I wrote this story.

However, the main inspiration comes from two sources. The first is the Olympics, which I love to watch on TV because it allows me to watch sports I never even think of most of the time, like archery and synchronised swimming – or weightlifting! Weightlifting is not a complicated sport, but it is full of drama. You can see how much it means to the competitors as they prepare themselves before a lift. It makes great material for a story. The other source was American all-in wrestling, which is full of larger-than-life characters in every sense. Many former sportsmen, quite often former weightlifters, become wrestlers. I merged the two sports in this story in McGower's character, he's a wrestler and he's a minor celebrity, too. So, although I respect weightlifting very much, I am not a dedicated fan because I only watch it during the Olympics.

Do you think that sports officials will ever be able to stop some sports people from cheating and taking drugs?

I am sure that the vast majority of sports competitors are honest, but there will always be people who want to win by other means. Drugs are becoming more subtle and difficult to detect. Plus there are always some unscrupulous people who try to plant drugs on innocent competitors. At the same time drugs testing facilities are becoming more efficient. Will they ever be able to prevent drug taking? I honestly don't know. Sometimes I wonder what would happen if they had two categories of sport: one for those who can take whatever performance-enhancing drug they want and another for those who don't take anything at all. It would be interesting to see the differences. One thing won't change, there will always be people who will do almost anything to win.

Sam Sullivan is a very sympathetic and often humorous narrator. How did you find his voice?

Sam is, essentially, an uncomplicated man who sees his coach both as a guide and father-figure. He sometimes expresses himself in quite an articulate way, which he probably would not be able to do if he were really stupid, which, of course, he isn't. I suppose I had in mind Bertie Wooster, the P. G. Wodehouse character who relies on his much cleverer butler, Jeeves, to sort out his troubles. They have a similar relationship, but the influence on my story was a subconscious one and not a deliberate decision.

I find, too, that using first-person narrative works well when writing humorous stories. It allows you to use a particular point of view or voice, and this makes the reading experience more intimate because it invites increased sympathy with the narrator.

You've created a really horrible villain in McGower. Is he based on anyone you know?

No, thank goodness! McGower is really a caricature based on the gangster films I watched as a boy. In these films the real villain usually had a huge, stupid partner to do his dirty work for him. Other influences are the 'bad guys' of the American wrestling circuit and Bugs Bunny's muscular opponents in the cartoons. I'm certainly not suggesting that weightlifters are at all like these characters. Indeed, I'm sure that there are numerous examples of lifters who have high IQs and work for charitable organisations in their spare time. But Duncan McGower isn't one of them.

In this story I felt it was important to have an opponent for Sam who was in many respects his opposite in character, who represents all the things Sam is not.

You've written and published many short stories. What is it that you particularly like about the short story genre?

From a selfish point of view, it takes a lot less time to write than a novel! I have also written study guides to collections of short stories for literature students, so it's a genre I am familiar with. I like the way that one can concentrate on a single character or situation. You can even focus on a single aspect of a character: in my case, I often bring out the fault or virtue in a character, which brings about the dénouement of the story. It's a bit like an artist working on a small, fine miniature rather than a large and elaborate fresco. I also like to use short stories as a way of exploring thought-provoking ideas, for example in science-fiction stories, where particular philosophical and moral questions might be raised.

Finally, as a reader it's often satisfying to have a piece of literature that you can read comfortably in one sitting.

Before Reading

Ⓐ Read the opening line of the story then write down:

Who you think is speaking
Why s/he is saying this
What kind of story you think this is going to be

Ⓑ Which of the following words is the odd man out (i.e. not the same as the others)?

competition	☐	banana	☐
championship	☐	fruit	☐
contest	☐	grape	☐
coach	☐	orange	☐

Ⓒ 'Coach often refers to Duncan McGower as some kind of animal.' The narrator describes several of the characters in terms of animals. What animal would you choose to describe yourself? Why?

Ⓓ 'There will always be people who will do almost anything to win,' says the author of this story. Do you agree? Give your reasons for or against.

Fruit Cocktail

I hate bananas.

Now I know they're supposed to be good for me – my coach* insists I eat them before every competition – but I've always hated the taste and even the sight of them. They're all yellow, with brown, blotchy* bits, like a squashed* caterpillar*. Yes, yes, I know they're perfect for giving a quick fix* of energy – all weightlifters eat energy food* before they do their stuff* – but why my coach insists on bananas is beyond me*. Especially after I got stuck* in a wheelchair for a whole month, after I slipped on one of the damn things.

I remember exactly when it happened. Some litter lout* dropped a banana skin on the pavement outside the stadium* and I missed the Regional Heavyweight Weightlifting Finals. Oh, the sickening* feeling when I suddenly fell forward and the awful pain as my left knee hit the concrete*! When you're my weight, a fall like that is no joke*.

I wish Coach liked oranges. They're sweet and tasty*, and good for you, too. I like oranges.

And I could have won that competition, too. I would have won. Coach hates me losing. Still, as I didn't take part in the finals, you couldn't say I lost, could you? But Coach didn't see it that way*. As far as Coach is

coach: sports trainer
blotchy: with small dark marks
squashed: pressed flat
caterpillar: small, long animal with many legs that becomes a butterfly or moth
quick fix: sudden amount of energy, like the effect of a drug
energy food: food eaten to give you energy
stuff: (here) what they do
beyond me: something I can't imagine
got stuck: was confined to, had to stay in
litter lout: someone who drops things on the ground and leaves them
stadium: large sports arena surrounded by seats
sickening: that makes you feel sick
concrete: material (cement, sand, stones and water) used to make pavements and buildings
no joke: not amusing
tasty: good to eat
didn't see it that way: did not have the same opinion

concerned*, if you're not a winner you're a loser, and that's that*.

"Sam Sullivan, you should be regional champion by now! Why did you have to go and slip on a banana skin? I should send you to the circus – they could use clowns like you there."

That's Coach for you* – never lost for* a few words of encouragement*. Anyway, I made up for lost time* once I was back on my feet again* and took* the English Championship the next time around*. "About time, too*," Coach said. I could tell he was delighted.

I don't look like Arnold Schwarzenegger – he's a bodybuilder*, and the whole point of being a bodybuilder is to show off* your muscles. They sometimes show muscles I never even knew existed . And they have no fat. They're like slabs* of marble* – all solid and sculpted*. Coach always says:

"Bodybuilders may look like Superman, but if you want to lift weights like Superman, you gotta* look like a truck*. So eat your bananas."

I *do* look like a truck. But I sure can lift weights.

I've always had strength, even when I was a kid. I'm not stupid, either,

as far as Coach is concerned: what Coach thinks
that's that: there is nothing more to say
that's Coach for you: that is what Coach is like
never lost for: never without
encouragement: that make you feel better
made up for lost time: reduced the negative effect caused by the time lost
back on my feet again: better, well
took: won
next time around: on the next occasion
about time, too: at last
bodybuilder: someone who develops their muscles as much as possible
show off: make people admire
slabs: thick flat pieces (usually of something hard)
marble: hard white stone
sculpted: shaped with care
you gotta: you've got to
truck: heavy lorry

though I'm no rocket scientist*. "Maximise your assets*" is what Coach always told me. So I maximised my assets and now I'm in with a real chance at the European All-Comers Weightlifting Championship Final. That's what Coach says. I'm the English champion and one of the favourites.

But I'm not the only one. My only real rival* is Duncan McGower, known to his fans as The Scottish Tower. He's from Glasgow. He *is* big – even bigger than me, and that's saying something*. He's so big he can look down on my bald spot*. He'd spit* on it, too, if I let him. He's as mean as they come*, but when they handed out brains, he must have been at the back of the queue*.

"He's got no quality," says Coach about my rival, "no style, no class. He may be bigger, Sam, but you've got built-in* quality – you're a natural*. There's nothing natural about the Tower, if you know what I mean."

I do know what he means. He means that Duncan McGower has enough steroids* in him to stock* a small hospital. You can tell. He looks like Hercules* and has a voice like Minnie Mouse*. Don't tell me that's natural. The trouble is, he always passes the drugs check – his blood and urine have always been as clean as a whistle*. But everyone knows. We don't know how he's fooled* the officials, but he's fooled

no rocket scientist: (slang) not very clever
maximise your assets: make the most of what you have
rival: person one competes against
that's saying something: (here) I'm big, so he must be huge
bald spot: area on the head without hair
spit: send liquid out of the mouth
as mean as they come: really bad
when they handed ... queue: he's very stupid
built-in: that is part of him
a natural: someone who has a natural talent
steroids: drugs that make muscles grow more quickly and make people stronger
stock: fill
Hercules: hero of Greek legend, famous for his incredible strength
Minnie Mouse: girlfriend of the cartoon character, Mickey Mouse
clean as a whistle: completely free of drugs
fooled: cheated

them somehow. It's been done before.

Now McGower is just too stupid to fix it* himself, so we've always reckoned* his coach, Spike Munroe, must be the brains behind* the whole thing. Spike is a big guy* with a small ratty* face and long, rodent-like* hands. Not the kind of person you'd take home for tea and biscuits, but he is a successful coach.

"You're the new boy," Coach warns me. "You're the only real competition the Tower's got. If it wasn't for you, he'd walk away with* this championship. But you're better than he is, Sam, and he knows it!"

In that case, I suggest, we've got no worries.

"Worries? We've got plenty of worries! That rat-faced, no-good Spike is gonna* try something, I'm sure of it. And as for that gorilla of his . . ."

Coach often refers to Duncan McGower as some kind of animal. Understandably.

"Now don't cross him*," Coach cautions* me. "The Tower's as mean as a bear with a sore* head, and he'd love to start an argument with you. And before you say it, I know you're not afraid of him, but if you get in a fight, you'll be in no shape* for the competition afterwards. And you could get disqualified*. So stay nice*. Now eat your banana."

fix it: organise it
reckoned: thought
the brains behind: the person with intelligence who runs something
guy: man
ratty: like a rat
rodent-like: like a rat or mouse
walk away with: win easily
gonna: going to
cross him: make him angry
cautions: warns
sore: that hurts
in no shape: not fit for
disqualified: thrown out of the competition
stay nice: behave well

How come Coach calls the Tower a gorilla, but I get the bananas?

....

The day of the Championships arrived and I had taken great care to keep out of the way of both the Tower and his coach. Not that they didn't try to provoke* me – getting me disqualified would have suited them just fine. But the Tower couldn't be subtle* if the word 'subtle' was tattooed* on his eyeballs. No, good old-fashioned* brute force* was more his style*, and it was always easy to see it coming, so I made sure I was never around if he so much as sneezed in my direction.

The competition was tougher than any of us had thought. There were a lot of strong guys out there and all of them wanted to take the title. Finally it was down to the last three: Massimo Verdi, the Italian champion, who was like a walking forklift truck*, McGower, who was lifting weights like an elephant lifting peanuts and – of course – me.

I was lifting like a dream*. I knew I couldn't fail, not if I kept my concentration.

Massimo Verdi dropped his final lift. The huge weights fell with the clang* of fallen anvils* and rolled off the stand*, nearly crushing a television cameraman who had the sense to abandon* his camera and

provoke: do something to deliberately annoy someone
subtle: delicate; that is not noticed
tattooed: drawn on the skin with needles
good old-fashioned: simple; the way things used to be
brute force: use of strength without thought
his style: his way of doing things
forklift truck: vehicle used in factories to lift heavy weights
like a dream: so well it felt as if I was dreaming
clang: sound of metal when it falls
anvils: heavy iron blocks on which metal is shaped
stand: raised area for performance
abandon: leave

jump out of the way. When hc picked up his camera again to continue, we all gave him a round of applause*, even Massimo, though he knew he was out of the contest. He's a good sport*, Massimo.

I couldn't say the same about the Tower. He was due to* lift his final weight next. Genghis Khan* was a sportsman compared to him.

I hadn't completed my final lift yet, which was OK because I was level with McGower so far. All I had to do to win the contest was lift a little bit over whatever the Tower lifted. Simple.

At least, that was the plan.

Then the Tower went to lift his weights. When they announced the weight he was going to attempt*, I couldn't believe it. He was going for a lift that was just under the world record! Now you don't do that unless you are actually in the World Championships – which we were not. Even worse, I wasn't ready to lift that much yet – the World Championships were almost eight months away. I knew McGower was a gorilla, but this would make him King Kong* – if he could do it.

I was so nervous that I even found myself chewing* a banana.

All eyes were on the Tower. He was like one of those old Greek statues as he stood staring angrily at the weights. Then he took hold of the

round of applause: we clapped him
good sport: someone who accepts defeat in a cheerful way
due to: expected to, about to
Ghengis Khan: 13th century figure whose name is associated with fierceness and cruelty
attempt: try
King Kong: huge gorilla in an American film
chewing: eating

bar*. Every huge muscle on his carefully manufactured* body stood out* as the weights were raised above his knees, then above his chest. Would he get them right up into the air? He gave a great shout – if that's the right word for a soprano voice like his – and raised the weights above his head. He stood for the required amount of time with a twisted grin* on his ugly face as we all watched.

In order for the lift to be allowed*, you have to have both arms straight at the elbow once the weight is raised. If one of the three judges thinks your elbows are not 'locked', as they say, your lift is not allowed. Three white lights are displayed for a good lift. If a red light shows, the lift does not count*.

Duncan McGower got one red light.

I have never seen anyone as mad* as he was that night. He let the weights drop, then kicked them aside* with his foot. They would have rolled onto somebody if Massimo and another lifter hadn't caught them. The Tower stormed off* like a wounded* buffalo, yelling* in his high voice that the judges must have been blind and doubting that the parents of at least one judge had been married. Or words to that effect*. That finally did it* as far as the judges were concerned. He was disqualified for "unsporting behaviour". Both he and Spike Munroe objected* to this 'unreasonable' decision. Munroe spat at one judge

bar: metal stick holding the weights
manufactured: made (i.e. by taking steroids)
stood out: were pushed out and could be seen
twisted grin: uneven smile
be allowed: qualify for the competition
does not count: is disqualified
mad: furious; very angry
aside: to one side
stormed off: left angrily
wounded: hurt; injured
yelling: shouting loudly
words to that effect: words with the same meaning
did it: it was that act which made the judges decide to disqualify him
objected: complained about

while the Tower jumped up and down in protest* before the delighted photographers. Then he snatched* somebody's camera and jumped up and down on that, too.

I was declared* the winner, though few people noticed in all the commotion*.

"Well, we were certainly lucky that time," said Coach when we finally got back to our dressing room.

"What do you mean?" I asked, as if I didn't know.

"I mean that damned ox McGower nearly had us beat*. If his technique* hadn't been so sloppy*, he'd have lifted that last weight. It's lucky for us he's so dumb*."

Coach had a point*. The Tower had all the skill and technique of a charging* rhinoceros. My technique, on the other hand, was good. Coach has always said I wasn't bad. And when Coach says somebody isn't bad, he means he's good. Very good. But even I would have had trouble with the weight McGower had lifted.

"Yes, you might have managed it, son," Coach commented. "But you'd have done yourself some kind of injury. In six months you'll be ready

in protest: to show that they disagreed
snatched: grabbed; took quickly and suddenly
declared: they said that I was
commotion: noise and confusion
had us beat: (slang) nearly beat us
technique: the way one does something
sloppy: not done well or carefully
dumb: stupid
had a point: was probably right
charging: running angrily towards something

for it, and more," he continued. "But how did McGower do it? He must have had some assistance, if I know Spike Munroe."

By "assistance" Coach meant that the Tower must have had enough steroids in him to sink a battleship*. But surely, even Spike Munroe wouldn't have been able to hide that from the officials. Would he? After watching the Tower's bad lifting technique, Coach wondered if Munroe really cared just how his man won, just so long as he did win. But how did he get away with it*? The Tower, of course, was too stupid to plot* anything – all he wanted to do was to win. What was Munroe up to*? Was he trying to prove to us that the Tower could win the World Championships his way and that there was nothing we could do about it?

I was worried.

The World Championships were just eight months away. Duncan McGower had, like me, already lifted enough to qualify. Coach had a theory*. He thought that Munroe was getting the Tower ready to go professional, and for that he needed publicity. Their recent behaviour had certainly got them that – lots of people would flock* to the competitions just to see what the bad boy* of the weightlifting world would do next. Coach also thought that was why Munroe was taking the risk of filling his man with steroids. Of course, so far he hadn't been found out, though no-one could work out why. It was the only way he could beat me, and he had to beat me to win.

battleship: ship used in war
get away with it: succeed in not being discovered
plot: plan
up to: planning
theory: something you think is possible, but have not yet proved
flock: come in crowds
bad boy: man with a reputation for behaving badly

Me and, of course, the current* World Champion – Uri Bolshoi, the Russian Bear.

Six months after the European All-Comers Championship I was heavily into* my training for the World Heavyweight Weightlifting title. I had improved. I had more than improved – I was great. Weights I would not have dared to lift before were now a part of my routine*. It was all down to* Coach. I may not have always appreciated* his methods: "This will hurt me more than it hurts you" was one of his favourite sayings. Why didn't I believe him, I wonder? But now I appreciated the results.

I still didn't appreciate the bananas, though. If I ate any more bananas, I was going to start climbing trees and watching Tarzan* films. "You'll thank me for it one day", Coach promised. Of course I would, but not in this life. Not that I'd ever dare say that to Coach, of course.

I managed to keep well clear of* Duncan McGower during this time. Well, most of the time. Occasionally, when we were in the same town, I would sneak into* the gym where he was training to see how he was doing. It isn't easy to sneak anywhere when you're my size, but there were plenty of other lifters sneaking around, too. In fact, as his training was open to the public and the press, there were more people around the Tower than ever.

current: existing; of today
heavily into: very busy doing
routine: what one does on a regular basis
down to: due to
appreciated: liked
Tarzan: character left in African jungle who grew up with apes
well clear of: away from
sneak into: go into a place without being seen

McGower had become something of a celebrity* since he had been disqualified in that last contest. People loved to hate him. And, let's face it*, it wasn't hard to do. Spike Munroe took full advantage of the situation. He had started using the Tower in TV commercials* for cereals* ("I eat crushed wheat to build up my meat*") and as the monster in some low-budget movies*. Wrestling organisations wanted him to join them because the bad guys always drew* the crowds. If badness were a measure* of popularity, they'd need a football stadium for all the Tower's fans. It seemed that Coach's theory might be right.

The only good thing I could see about Spike Munroe's training methods was his use of oranges. Most coaches recommend some kind of food to give you a quick burst* of energy. My coach had bananas – Spike Munroe used oranges. And I love oranges. However, I could see from the look on his ugly face that McGower hated oranges as much as I hated bananas.

It's funny how things work out in life, isn't it?

Anyway, there I was watching the Tower from the back of the gym. I had been trying to mix in with the crowd, but it didn't work*. He put down his weights and pointed at me, saying in his silly voice: "Sullivan, I can see you! I'm going to beat you! You're never gonna see that world title. I'm gonna win it!"

Clever remarks were not one of the Tower's strong points*.

celebrity: someone who is famous
let's face it: it's unpleasant, but true
commercials: advertisements on television
cereals: breakfast food like muesli
build up my meat: make me strong
low-budget movies: films made for very little money
drew: attracted
measure: a way of measuring
burst: sudden amount
didn't work: was not successful
strong points: most positive qualities

I decided to fight fire with fire*. Quick as a flash*, I shouted back to him: "We'll see about that*!"

It was not exactly witty* repartee*, but it certainly got a reaction from the Tower. His face turned purple and his mouth twisted into a mask of anger. He ran towards me with one huge fist* raised, photographers giving way* before him like waves before a ship in full sail*.

I didn't want to fight him just before the World Championships. I'd be in no shape* for the contest after that. But I had nowhere to turn. I didn't know what to do. He was charging towards me like a wild animal with a bad attitude. "Goodbye championships, hello hospital," I thought.

You know how it is in films when the good guy is in a tight spot* and then, all of a sudden*, he's saved by something unexpected? Well, I certainly didn't expect what happened next.

All of a sudden, a giant figure stepped between the Tower and me. He wasn't any taller than McGower, but he seemed to be twice as wide. This giant stood there like a great oak tree with his hands on his hips and his thick legs rooted to the ground*.

It was Uri Bolshoi, the Russian Bear. The World Champion.

fight fire with fire: respond to attack by attacking
quick as a flash: very quickly
see about that: I'll do something to stop that happening
witty: clever and funny
repartee: quick amusing conversation
fist: closed hand
giving way: making space for him to go past
in full sail: with all its sails up, (i.e. moving quickly)
in no shape: unfit
tight spot: difficult situation
all of a sudden: suddenly
rooted to the ground: standing without moving

It's difficult for a large man to stop quickly when he's charging full ahead. But when the Tower saw Uri Bolshoi standing in front of him, something must have clicked in his tiny brain, because he stopped. He looked at Bolshoi and his face couldn't decide between anger and fear.

It chose fear.

Uri Bolshoi looked straight at the Tower and said: "Go back!"

That's all. Nothing else. But the Tower got the message. He turned around and crept* back to the waiting arms of Spike Munroe, who had plenty* to say to him, most of which was unrepeatable*. The Russian Bear turned to me and smiled. "I don't like him!" he said. It was right then that I decided I liked Uri Bolshoi. He was OK by me.

Coach and I were feeling lucky. For a start, the World Championships were being held in Manchester this year, which is not far from us. The home crowd* would be there to cheer us on, and that is always an advantage.

Then there was the surprise announcement by the Russian team that Uri Bolshoi was retiring from competitive lifting. He wanted to become a trainer, like Coach. Coach knew Uri, though not well. Nobody knew him well. But everyone respected him. Uri Bolshoi had been champion for years. In the past he had been the man to fear, the man to beat.

crept: moved slowly and quietly
plenty: lots of things
unrepeatable: that cannot be repeated because it is rude
home crowd: local supporters, fans

It would have been a great achievement* for me to beat him because he had been the best for so long. Uri was terrifyingly big, but he seemed to have a good heart and always encouraged younger lifters.

Still, I won't say his retirement wasn't a relief to us. It was. Realistically*, Uri had been my only real rival for the title. The Tower, I knew in my heart, would never be as good as me. Now, unless something went badly wrong, the title was sure to be mine.

Of course, if I'd known then how things were going to turn out, this could have been a different story ...

At last, the day of the World Championships arrived. The stadium was packed* with fans from all over the world.

The heavyweight events were not until late in the day, giving us all plenty of time to get really nervous and wound up*. The Russians had won many of the lighter weight categories*, which was just as well because they had no real contenders in the heavyweight division now that Uri had stood down*.

It would soon be my turn to lift. I found myself sitting on the bench peeling* my usual banana while Coach was exchanging tips* with Uri Bolshoi, whose English was a lot better than our Russian. Coach said it was a lot better than my English, too. He was joking. I think.

achievement: something really great
realistically: it is true to say
packed: full
wound up: nervous
categories: groups
stood down: retired from the sport
peeling: taking off the skin
exchanging tips: giving and receiving useful ideas

Anyway, there I was, watching Massimo Verdi begin the contest by lifting the weight of a small elephant above his head, when Duncan McGower walked up and sat next to me. He was holding an orange. I decided to ignore him. I was too nervous to worry about him just then. All at once he turned to me with something that looked like a smile on his face. It was not a pretty sight*, but somehow I managed to smile back.

He looked at my banana. I looked at his orange. Well, it was better than looking at him.

Finally, he spoke. "Hey, do you want to swap* your banana for my orange?"

not a pretty sight: ugly

swap: exchange

As an opening to a conversation, it did not have the stamp of greatness*. I replied, choosing my words with careful consideration*.

"OK."

We exchanged fruit and ate in silence. Actually, he was far from silent as he made short work* of my banana, but he didn't actually speak. He watched me as I swallowed the last segment of the orange, then smiled again and got up.

"Thanks," he said, then walked back to Spike Munroe, who waved his long, ratty hand and smiled at me. They were both smiling now.

It was scary*.

"You did *what*!"

Coach had smelled the orange and saw some of the peel* on the bench next to me. I told him what had happened. I didn't see the harm in it*. It was only an orange. I like oranges.

"Let's hope you're right, and it really was just an orange," said Coach, half to himself.

it did not have the stamp of greatness: it wasn't very clever or memorable
careful consideration: carefully
made short work: do something quickly (i.e. ate it fast)
scary: frightening
peel: skin
harm in it: that I'd done anything wrong

I asked him what he meant.

"Never mind. But don't leave my side for the rest of the competition – right?" ordered Coach. It wasn't like Coach to sound so worried. He often sounded annoyed, but he rarely sounded worried, not this worried.

An official indicated that it was my turn to begin lifting. Coach did his best to sound cheerful again. " Now come on Sam," he said encouragingly. "You've got a competition to win!"

....

The competition went exactly as everybody had expected. Massimo Verdi, Duncan McGower and me were the last three lifters in a very tough* contest. Each of us had our supporters, but Massimo's and mine were all weightlifting fans. The Tower's fans included some weightlifting enthusiasts, but there were also a lot of extra people who had been drawn by all the publicity. There seemed to be hundreds of them. They cheered the Tower when he made a lift and booed* the rest of us. We didn't like the sound of it.

Massimo was the first to go down*. He lifted like a hero, but sprained* his back and had to retire. He got a tremendous* cheer*, even from the new crowd. It was hard not to like Massimo.

Now it was all down to me and the Tower*. We each had two lifts to go.

tough: difficult; hard
booed: sound of dislike (boo) from spectators
go down: fail
sprained: injured by twisting
tremendous: huge
cheer: clap and shout in approval
down to . . . Tower: we were the last two

The Tower was first.

He seemed to be bigger than ever. He looked as if somebody had taken a large tyre-pump to him and had forgotten to stop inflating. He was like a giant sumo wrestler*.

The weight he had chosen was truly enormous*. It would be a new world record. He rubbed his hands with chalk dust to get a better grip* and took hold of the bar to begin the lift.

The heavy bar that supported the weights bent as he raised it to his knees – but it held*. The Tower's face went dark and his eyes stared with the strain* as he lifted the bar to his shoulders. Then he began to lift it over his head. His arms shook with the effort until, at last, he raised the bar. This time his arms were straight.

The lift was good. He got three white lights.

He had broken the world record!

The stadium* went wild*, but then went quiet again as my lift was announced. Coach had told me that I had to decide. Should I go for an even heavier weight? For me there was only one answer. I couldn't let Coach down. I asked for an extra kilo on the bar.

But first I had a banana, just to keep Coach happy.

sumo wrestler: Japanese wrestler
enormous: huge
grip: hold (on something)
held: (here) did not break
strain: effort
the stadium: the crowd in the stadium
went wild: cheered loudly and without control

It's hard to remember now what happened next, but it seemed that all there was to life in those few moments of lifting was pain. I knew it was over when I dropped the weights after the white lights showed and the crowds started cheering. Even the new crowd cheered me.

I had broken the new world record!

The Tower, of course, immediately tried an even heavier lift. But he didn't get it as far as his knees. In fact, he sprained his shoulder in the attempt and couldn't lift again. He hadn't sprained his mouth, though, and he let everybody know it. He cursed and swore*, but it was no good. All eyes were on me.

Including those of the medical officials. That rat, Munroe, was having a heated discussion* with them and pointing in my direction while holding the remains* of my orange peel in his other rodent-like hand.

However, it was too late for Munroe to stop me from being awarded* the gold medal*. I can't say I wasn't proud as the medal was placed around my neck. McGower took the silver but, of course, his shoulder was injured and they couldn't place it over his neck. So he had to hold it. He was not a gracious* loser and whispered his colourful opinions* of my success to me as we stood together on the rostrum*.

cursed and swore: said bad words
heated discussion: argument
remains: what was left
awarded: given
medal: award given to winners
gracious: behaving in a nice, polite way
his colourful opinions: rudely said what he thought
rostrum: raised area where the medal-winners stand

Massimo Verdi was in the treatment room* having his back seen to*, but he still got cheered for coming third.

The funny thing is, as the Tower was breathing into my ear, all I could think of was the taste of the banana I had eaten. It had taken away all the taste of the orange.

As I said, life is funny sometimes.

Following a complaint from Munroe, I had my blood tested and the officials found steroids in it – the same steroids that had been found in the orange. No wonder* Munroe and McGower had been smiling when I ate it. The orange had been absolutely stuffed* with a cocktail of steroids and other banned* drugs which Munroe had put in it, just as Coach had suspected.

I was stripped of* the title straight after winning it.

That was not, however, the end of the story.

I saw Coach and Uri Bolshoi deep in conversation*. Uri thought he'd seen Spike Munroe somewhere before and he'd done some checking. Munroe had once worked as a biochemist in Russia. That's where Uri had seen him, backstage* at a local competition, talking to local coaches, trying to sell drugs.

treatment room: place for medical care
seen to: treated
no wonder: it wasn't surprising that
stuffed: filled
banned: illegal; forbidden
stripped of: it was taken away from me
deep in conversation: talking together attentively
backstage: the area behind a stage

Munroe's real name, it turned out, was Gregor Pushkin. He'd once been a brilliant scientist and had invented a way of eliminating* all traces* of drugs from the body within twenty-four hours of their being taken. However, the drug you had to take to achieve this had side-effects: if you used it too often, it made you lose 'intellectual efficiency'*. In other words, you became stupid. Not that anyone had noticed any great change in Duncan McGower!

Munroe had left Russia pretty quickly when officials started to investigate him. He'd changed his name and carried on with his experiments in Britain. Coach came and told me the news.

"But Coach," I said. "That doesn't help us– the Tower must have taken that stuff well before the contest. He'll be clean as a whistle again, like he always is."

"Wanna bet*?" said Coach with a grin. He explained that Uri had arranged for Munroe to be spied on*. After Uri discovered how Munroe had put drugs into the orange McGower had given me, he decided to carry out a little plan of his own. He got one of his helpers to secretly add something to the Tower's own oranges, something from a bottle which Uri had taken from Munroe's bag.

Coach, like the honest citizen he is, was then sent to inform* the

eliminating: getting rid of
traces: signs
'intellectual efficiency': the ability to think clearly
wanna bet: do you want to bet (gamble) on it?
spied on: secretly watched
inform: tell

officials that he had reason to believe that McGower was using illegal substances. Very soon afterwards, McGower's blood and urine were checked, and he was quickly stripped of his new medal.

Not only was Duncan McGower declared guilty of taking drugs; he was the first man ever in the history of weight-lifting competitions to be declared pregnant! Don't ask me how, but Munroe had been stealing hormones* from the maternity unit* of the city hospital.

It was too late for me because the other stuff* was in my blood. Even though everybody acknowledged that I was innocent, the rules were the rules. But it was good news for Massimo – they told him in hospital that he was the new champion.

Good old Massimo!

I knew that I'd lifted those weights through my own ability – those drugs hadn't been long enough in my body to make any difference. And, as Coach says, there's always a next time. But still . . .

Funny thing is I've gone off oranges, too. Now I hate the taste of bananas *and* oranges. And I'm going to tell Coach, I don't care what he says.

Maybe he'll let me eat grapes.

I like grapes.

hormones: chemicals in the body that affect growth and development

maternity unit: where babies are born

stuff: (here) drugs

After Reading

Response

Ⓐ Sam accepted the loss of his World Championship title because 'rules were rules'. Do you think the judges were fair? Why? Why not? You may wish to use an example from real life in your answer.

Ⓑ Which of the following adjectives best describe the story?

funny	☐	tragic	☐	sad	☐	frightening	☐
strange	☐	exciting	☐	surprising	☐		

Ⓒ What was your first impression of Sam? Did you like him more or less as the story continued?

Comprehension

Ⓐ Place the following into chronological order.

I got stuck in a wheelchair.	☐
I suddenly fell forward.	☐
I missed the Regional Heavyweight Weightlifting Finals.	☐
Some litter lout dropped a banana skin on the pavement.	☐
My left knee hit the concrete.	☐

Ⓑ Which of the following describe McGower and which Spike Munroe?

	McGower	Munroe
He's so big	☐	☐
mean as they come	☐	☐
voice like Minnie Mouse	☐	☐
long rodent-like hands	☐	☐

After Reading

Ⓒ Who did what? Complete by matching the following actions to the correct characters:

.... nearly crushed a TV cameraman.
.... was lifting weights like an elephant lifting peanuts.
.... went for a lift just under the world record.
.... started chewing a banana.
.... gave a great shout.
.... was lifting like a dream.
.... caught the weights.
.... objected to the judges' decision.
.... declared Sam the winner.

Ⓓ What does Coach mean when he says that McGower 'must have had some assistance'?

Ⓔ 'It seemed that Coach's theory might be right.' Which of the following was Coach's theory?

- The Tower wanted to sell breakfast cereal. ☐
- Munroe wanted the Tower to become a celebrity. ☐
- Munroe wanted to become a celebrity. ☐
- The Tower wanted more fans. ☐

Ⓕ Who or what is being described in the following phrases?

his face turned purple
had nowhere to turn
like a wild animal with a bad attitude
stood there like a great oak tree
like waves before a ship in full sail

After Reading

Ⓖ Which of the following statements are True and which are False?

	True	False
Uri Bolshoi decided to retire from competitive lifting.	☐	☐
Coach knew Uri Bolshoi very well.	☐	☐
Everyone was afraid of Uri.	☐	☐
Uri always encouraged young weightlifters.	☐	☐
Uri decided to become a coach.	☐	☐

Ⓗ '"Let's hope you're right, and it really was just an orange," said Coach.' What did Coach mean, and why were Spike and the Tower smiling?

Ⓘ Read the following sports commentary and fill in the missing gaps.

And here comes the Tower! He seems bigger every year and now let's see what weight he's chosen . . . he's chosen a really enormous weight. If he gets this, it will be a new .... He's got the .... in his hands. He's lifting it. Yes! His arms are .... The judges have given him three .... lights. He's done it! He's .... the world record and the stadium is going .... And now here comes Sam. He's looking good and he's chosen to add another kilo. Can he do it? He's in pain, but he's done it! It's a new world record and the crowds are .... I've never seen anything like this!

Ⓙ Who was Munroe, where did he come from and what experiments was he carrying out in Britain?

Ⓚ Who won the World Championship in the end and how?

After Reading

Plot and Setting

Ⓐ The story is in nine sections (separated by dotted lines). Give each section a title. For example you could call the first section 'Introducing Sam'.

Ⓑ The story is about the rivalry between Sam and the Tower. What role does Uri Bolshoi play in their battle for the Championship?

Ⓒ What do you think is the climax of the story? Does the story end there? If not, what happens afterwards?

Ⓓ Imagine you are making a film of the story. How many settings would you need? Describe them.

Ⓔ The author does not always say where things are taking place. Does this matter? Give your reasons why/why not.

Theme

Ⓐ Which of the following sentences do you think best describes the theme of the story?

- Winning isn't everything; what is important is how you play the game. ☐
- The only important thing is to win; it doesn't matter how you do it. ☐
- Win or lose – there's always another day. ☐
- The world loves a winner. ☐

Ⓑ 'If badness were a measure of popularity, they'd need a football stadium for all the Tower's fans.'
Why did the Tower get so many new fans when he behaved so badly? Do you think they were right to support him?

Narration and Style

Ⓐ The style of the author is very colloquial and informal, and Sam seems to be talking to the reader. Can you think of any other stories which use this technique?

Ⓑ Find five examples in the text where Sam addresses the reader directly and say what effect this creates.

Ⓒ A great deal of the humour in Sam's narrative is produced by exaggeration ('McGower . . . was lifting weights like an elephant lifting peanuts.') or by deliberate understatement ('He was not a gracious loser.' i.e. he was a very bad loser). Which of the following sentences is an example of exaggerated speech (E) and which is a humorous understatement (H)?

	E	H
McGower has enough steroids in him to stock a small hospital.	☐	☐
Not the kind of person you'd take home for tea and biscuits.	☐	☐
He's as mean as a bear with a sore head.	☐	☐
He couldn't be subtle if the word 'subtle' was tattooed on his eyeballs.	☐	☐
Clever remarks were not one of the Tower's strong points.	☐	☐
I'm no rocket scientist.	☐	☐
Genghis Khan was a sportsman compared to him.	☐	☐

After Reading

Character

Ⓐ Sam says: 'I'm not stupid...though I'm no rocket scientist.' Do you agree? Find examples to support your argument.

Ⓑ All the characters in the story are very big. How has the author succeeded in giving them individual characteristics?

Ⓒ Sam describes other characters in terms of animals. How do you see Sam? And how do you think the other characters see him?

Vocabulary work

Ⓐ Match the following words or phrases.

heated	fix
a quick	spot
rocket	crowd
bald	*discussion*
a good	grin
twisted	scientist
strong	consideration
home	points
careful	sport

Ⓑ Make a list of all the animals mentioned in the story and write down the qualities you think are associated with each one. For example: an ox is big and strong.

After Reading

Ask the Author

Ⓐ Read the following statements and decide if they are True or False.

	True	False
The author used to be a weightlifter.	☐	☐
The author met several bodybuilders at his gym.	☐	☐
The story was inspired by the Olympics and American all-in wrestling.	☐	☐
Weightlifting is not a dramatic sport.	☐	☐
Many wrestlers were once weightlifters.	☐	☐

Ⓑ Answer the following questions.

1. Why was the author influenced by the stories of P. G. Wodehouse?
2. What were the three sources of inspiration for the character of Duncan McGower?
3. Does the author think that real weightlifters are like Duncan McGower?
4. According to the author, what is the effect on the reader of using a first-person narrator?

Ⓒ Which of the following qualities of short stories are mentioned by the author?

quicker to write	☐
quicker to read	☐
focus on a single character	☐
focus on a single event	☐
focus on a particular aspect of character	☐
like a miniature work of art	☐
like a short film	☐

After Reading

Follow-up

Speaking

In pairs imagine an interview with a member of the audience from the Weightlifting World Championship. One of you should ask the questions and the other give answers about what it was like and what happened.

Writing

Coach wrote a book about his experiences with Sam. Write an extract from this book.

Or

Design a poster advertising Sam's next appearance.

Class activity

Imagine that you – the class – are coaching a team for a world championship (in any sport). Create a fitness programme that includes:

- information and advice on diet
- a timetable for training
- notes on the psychology of winning

ANTOINETTE MOSES

The Cleopatra *Club*

About the Author

Antoinette Moses has, among numerous other occupations, written all her life. She has been a journalist, an editor, a film festival director and a cook. She has published a guide to Athens, a guide to running arts festivals, a cookery book and a book of poetry, as well as six original EFL readers. She has also co-written the scripts for two EFL videos and has written a novel, a novel for children and four plays, one for BBC Radio 4. She has also written and presented two television series for Channel 4.

Ask the Author

Is the Cleopatra Club itself based on a real club?

No. I invented it, but the other clubs mentioned in the story do exist. After I wrote the story, I discovered there was a society called 'Women of Trinity'. This is a women-only club at Trinity College in Cambridge, which organises talks, supports women students and aims to increase awareness of women in the college and the university as a whole. Men can't be members, but they can attend events if they are brought along by a female member. This reverses the usual rules of men-only clubs, which was my idea in writing the story. Interestingly, new laws in England may mean that such rules have to change. Soon, clubs and societies will have to be only for men and women, or enable men and women to take part in every aspect of club life. These laws are being brought in to stop the current practices in English golf clubs, for example, where women are allowed to play golf, but not allowed to drink in the club bars.

Apart from the club itself, how much of the story is fictional and how much fact?

The story is fictional, but the setting is factual. The information about Trinity College is all true, and what the characters say about Footlights is also authentic.

There is a lot of detail about Cambridge. How do you know so much about it?

I lived in Cambridge for ten years. During that time I got to know the city very well because I ran a film festival and edited a 'what's on' magazine. And though I wasn't a student at Cambridge, many of my friends were, and I spent quite a lot of time there.

Do you share Sara's opinion that Cambridge University is really élitist?

This is a difficult question. In many ways the University does everything it can to be open to everyone. Entry to the university today – and this wasn't always true – is based on merit. You don't get into Cambridge just because one of your parents went there; you have to get very high grades in your exams. But Oxford and Cambridge – known collectively as Oxbridge – are different from other universities in England. They do attract many of the very best students. For example, Cambridge has the Cavendish Laboratories, where many Nobel prize-winners have worked and continue to work. This attracts students who dream of being Nobel prize-winners themselves.
When you are in Cambridge, you get a real sense of history, a sense of being in a very special place. The fact that the colleges are some of the most beautiful buildings in the country adds to this. Did you know there was another university in Cambridge? The Anglia Polytechnic University. Until a few years ago this was an art school and a polytechnic college combined. The students often find themselves working for the students in Cambridge University colleges, as suggested in the story. So, to answer the question, I think that Cambridge can feel élitist. Is it actually élitist? I leave the answer to that question to the reader.

Do you think that women need special clubs?

Possibly. Men use clubs to network and help each other, and therefore it seems sensible for women to do the same. The 'glass ceiling' that prevents women from getting the top management jobs is beginning to disappear, but it is a very slow process. Most of the chief executives in business are still men, and this situation will not change overnight. The same is true in many other professions, and in politics, even though Britain has had a woman Prime Minister – though she herself was famous for not supporting other women. I grew up fighting for equality at work. There was clear discrimination when I was younger, different rates of pay for men and women, and different opportunities. If women join clubs as students to work together and help each other, that has to be a good thing. But I don't believe in initiation ceremonies of any kind, and I'm very much against hazing in any form. I see it as a form of bullying and it should not be allowed.

Before Reading

Ⓐ What do you know about clubs? Tick the appropriate column.

	Always	Sometimes
Members share the same interests.	☐	☐
You have to pay to join.	☐	☐
Anyone can join.	☐	☐
Members join them to practise sports.	☐	☐
They are only for young people.	☐	☐

Ⓑ Read the first two sentences of the story. Why do you think that 'Rule 1' will annoy a lot of people?

Ⓒ Have you ever joined a club or society? As a class, make a list of all the clubs and societies you belong to.

Ⓓ Which of the following words and phrases are related to university life and which are related to the world of work? Which do you think can belong to both categories?

University	Work	Both

examination • politician • editor • supervision • scholarship
author • essay • entrepreneur • networking • producer
historian • collegiate • system • writer • social scientist
room-mate • teacher • professor • careers office • tutor

The Cleopatra Club

Rule 1: The Club will be open only to women.
That will annoy a lot of people.

Rule 2: The Club will be open to members of all Cambridge Colleges.
That's good.

Rule 3: Members of Cambridge University wishing to join the Cleopatra Club will have to satisfy* the committee as to their eligibility*. The Committee will select* members according to merit*. The judgement of the Committee is final. Those not selected cannot appeal* the decision.

Rule 4. The aims* of the Cleopatra Club are . . .

Caroline Kitson looked at her computer screen and sighed. This was hard. She knew what the aims of the Club were. The Club was her idea, her 'baby', as she put it. But she couldn't write down what she really wanted. The aims of the Cleopatra Club were, as far as she was concerned, to create an élite*. A new élite, made up entirely of women. She wanted to gather together all the women currently at Cambridge who were going to succeed: the next generation of politicians, newspaper editors and television producers. And she wanted to be at the centre, at the heart of this new élite. However, that wasn't the way to describe it to others.

She began again.

....

satisfy: persuade completely
eligibility: suitability to become members
select: choose
merit: individual quality
appeal: make a request to change a decision
aims: what it hopes to achieve
élite: small group of people who are (or think they are) superior to others

The idea of the Cleopatra Club had come to Caroline several weeks previously. She'd been sitting drinking cappuccino in the Trinity Café, looking at the posters on the walls for forthcoming* plays, poetry readings and the next Footlights* show. Outside she could see a group of Japanese tourists in colourful raincoats huddling* under umbrellas like lost birds in a storm. A guide was lecturing* them as they lined up* to go into Trinity College and view* the famous Wren Library, designed by the architect who had built St Paul's Cathedral in London. She could imagine the commentary*; she had heard it many times before under her study window:

"And this is Trinity College, one of Cambridge's thirty-one colleges, founded by Henry the Eighth in 1546. He was the one who had six wives and was the father of Elizabeth the First. Follow me under this arch* and you'll be following in the footsteps of famous Cambridge students such as the Earl of Essex, who Queen Elizabeth fell in love with, and who was a student here in the sixteenth century. There have been many famous students here at Trinity including the poets Dryden, Marvell, Byron – who was famous for keeping a bear in his rooms, nowadays no pets are allowed – and Tennyson. Trinity College is also famous for its scientists and thinkers such as Nobel prize-winner, Bertrand Russell, and Sir Isaac Newton, who discovered gravity* when an apple fell on his head. (Outside the college gate we shall see the tree that is a direct descendant* of Newton's apple tree.) Among past students at Trinity there are at least six prime ministers of Great Britain, an Irish president, one French prime minister, the founder of the Bank of England and two Indian prime ministers, including Nehru, India's first prime minister . . . and Caroline Kitson."

forthcoming: in the near future
Footlights: Cambridge University society that puts on comedy shows
huddling: grouped closely together
lecturing: giving them a talk about a topic
lined up: queued
view: see
commentary: words spoken by a guide
arch: curved shape formed above two columns, e.g. above a door
gravity: the force that makes things fall to the ground
direct descendant: (here) that comes from the original tree

Well, smiled Caroline to herself. Maybe one day that's what they'll say.

Everyone had always known that Caroline Kitson was special; ever since nursery school* her ability to draw people to her* had been noted by teachers and classmates alike. Those whom she accepted, the ones within her orbit*, thought she was wonderful; those she kept out – the rejected, the ones who didn't measure up* – had other thoughts. They kept these thoughts to themselves. It didn't do* to cross* Caroline Kitson. She had quiet, unseen ways of retribution*. Her mother knew this more than most. She could not understand how a quiet, unassuming* woman like herself could have given birth to this brilliant, assured* and uncompromising* girl. She had done her best* over the years to control Caroline.

nursery school: school for children aged two to five
draw . . . to her: attract
orbit: near her, her close friends
measure up: have enough good qualities to attract her
it didn't do: it wasn't a good idea
cross: go against; oppose
retribution: getting revenge
unassuming: not wanting to be noticed
assured: confident
uncompromising: not willing to change her mind or opinion
done her best: tried very hard

"You don't want to give her a swollen head*," she'd say when someone praised Caroline. "You're so sharp, you'll cut yourself*," she'd tell her daughter, when Caroline came up with the answer to something she'd been puzzling over*.

This could be almost anything from the total of her weekly shop* to why they kept changing the packaging* on her washing powder. "Because they want people to think it's different in some way. They want people to notice the box instead of just looking at it like wallpaper*."

Caroline had been eleven years old when she'd said this. Her mother had looked at her in amazement; it was a look Caroline never forgot. After that, the same look frequently crossed* her mother's face. "She's too clever by half*," her mother used to complain to her father. "You're getting too big for your boots*," was another favourite saying. Caroline's father merely laughed. He was astonished, yet delighted, by the cleverness of his daughter. He refused to believe that Caroline was as ruthless* as his wife said. Privately*, he wondered whether Caroline's mother was jealous of her bright daughter. But he said nothing and kept away from their rows*, which were frequent and loud.

Caroline grew up despising* her mother. The older she got, the more

give her a swollen head: make her arrogant and think she is better than others
so sharp you'll cut yourself: too quick and clever
puzzling over: trying to understand
weekly shop: the amount she spent on food every week
packaging: design of the box
wallpaper: something that is always there and that you don't notice
look . . . crossed: expression that briefly passed across
too clever by half: too clever
too big for your boots: behaving as if you are more important than you really are
ruthless: who will do anything to get what she wants
privately: to himself
rows: arguments
despising: having no respect for

she became convinced that she'd been adopted*, but the evidence was against it. There were the baby photographs, as well as pictures of her mother in the later stages of pregnancy*. Another teenage fantasy was that she had been swapped in the hospital at birth, but she was clearly her father's daughter. She had his red hair and his family nose, straight and strong. Caroline felt like a cuckoo* in an uncomfortably small nest; she didn't belong behind the nylon lace curtains of her parents' small suburban* house, with its scent of lavender* furniture polish* and their fear of upsetting* the neighbours.

"I expect you'll be finding a job and settling down* after you leave school," was the kind of remark she heard around her school friends' houses. Caroline smiled, but said nothing. She had no intention* of settling down. She was simply waiting to escape. And escape she did, as she had known she would.

At seventeen, Caroline won a scholarship to go to Trinity College at Cambridge University. At eighteen years and three months, she packed a large suitcase and got on a train to London, crossed the capital by herself – something her mother had never done – got on another train at King's Cross Station and arrived at Cambridge. The fact that it was a damp September day with a cold wind blowing in across the North Sea did nothing to freeze her spirits*. She was jubilant*. She had made it*. She was free.

adopted: brought up by parents who are not her natural parents
pregnancy: when Caroline was about to be born
cuckoo: bird that grows up in another bird's nest pushing out the mother's own baby chicks
suburban: residential area around a city, thought in Britain to be safe and middle-class but boring
lavender: purple flower with sweet perfume
polish: cream to make furniture shine
upsetting: annoying
settling down: finding a place you can stay for the rest of your life
intention: wish or plan
freeze her spirits: stop her being cheerful and happy
jubilant: extremely happy
made it: succeeded

Cambridge had lived up to her expectations*. And it wasn't just the college itself, where it felt as if generations of study had seeped into the stone walls*. No. Walking down narrow streets where the houses rose straight from the pavements like cliffs, Caroline saw that every house was packed with paintings and books. Books piled* on shelves, books piled on desks, books piled on tables. It was the world she had always dreamed of.

And on every street there were bookshops; bookshops with new books, books written by people living and working in Cambridge, and bookshops with second-hand books*. Caroline found books with messages inside their covers. "Dear PS, thought you might be interested in reviewing* this for the TLS," wrote the author in one.

Caroline clutched* the book tightly in her hands. It had belonged to the author, a writer she had admired for many years and now she was holding it. The author had sent it to someone called PS, perhaps a professor, and had hoped they would write a review in the Times Literary Supplement, a journal* she had only recently discovered. The fact that PS had tossed* the book aside and sold it to a second-hand bookshop gave the book a history and made it even more precious. Caroline bought the book; it became a talisman*. She would touch it for luck before going to read an essay to her tutor.

She never told this to anyone. She never mentioned to her new friends that she kept expecting someone to turn up* at her door and say there had been a mistake, she didn't belong there, in Cambridge, in this

expectations: everything she had hoped for
it felt . . . walls: it felt as if the walls contained all the learning of the past
piled: placed one on top of the other
second-hand books: old books
reviewing: writing about it
clutched: held
journal: literary magazine
tossed: thrown
talisman: something you have to bring you luck
turn up: arrive

college. She belonged in a street of houses with neat gardens and no books. She waited for the knock on her door, the person arriving to say that she had been found out, that she was an impostor*.

But nobody came and said this, and Caroline knew she wasn't alone in feeling like an impostor in this university. Other students said they felt the same. Only those who had gone to public schools* and whose parents had studied at Cambridge felt they had the right to be there*. For many others, although they knew that they had won a place* because of their intelligence and hard work, the university always felt just a bit intimidating*. Caroline's room-mate* Sara often said this.

Sara was a quiet girl, prettier than she thought she was, with soft brown hair and wide-set blue eyes. She had won a place to study history, which her father had studied at Trinity many years before and which her brother had studied at Oxford before he had gone abroad, before the accident. The car crash that her parents had never got over*. Sara tried hard to live up to his reputation*. Her brother, Rob, had been brilliant both as a student and a rugby player, and Sara had tried to get into a university hockey team when she arrived, but she wasn't quite good enough. Secretly, Sara hated Cambridge. She was sure that it wasn't her interview and examination results that had got her into Trinity, but the fact she was the daughter of a well-known historian. She felt she was living someone else's life, but she couldn't see any way to change the situation. She also thought the university was élitist*. Sara often chatted* to the girl who came every weekday to clean their room and make their beds.

impostor: someone who does not belong; fake
public schools: private schools
had . . . there: really belonged there
won a place: been accepted by the university
intimidating: frightening
room-mate: someone with whom you share a room
got over: recovered from
reputation: what he was known for
élitist: favouring a small group of élite
chatted: talked

"It's disgusting in this day and age*," Sara complained to Caroline. "Having bedmakers*. Even calling them that. It's archaic*. And Jill's a student herself, at Anglia Poly*. She just can't manage* on a student loan*."

"I know the feeling," smiled Caroline. "I wouldn't mind some paid work myself."

Sara nodded. She knew that apart from the scholarship from the College, Caroline didn't have any other money. Sara was lucky compared with so many other students: her parents helped out financially, but she still didn't feel comfortable having other students cleaning up after her or waiting on her at table*. It all added to her feelings of unease. The one thing which kept her going was her friendship with Caroline. Caroline was everything she wanted to be: assured, brilliant and pretty.

Caroline was content for Sara to be her friend. She took Sara around with her and Sara often found herself spending evenings with boys who hoped that she was a way of getting closer to Caroline. Sara never complained. At least she had company. She wasn't alone. And Caroline always made her feel special.

No-one knew that Caroline herself had doubts and fears. She was so assured, so clever, so popular, so successful. People asked her to parties and to join clubs; her tutors smiled when she came to read her essays; her work was always thoughtful and interesting. She was certain to get a first-class degree. Caroline was sure to be a success.

this day and age: now
bedmakers: someone in a Cambridge college who cleans rooms and makes the beds
archaic: old-fashioned; not something that should happen today
Poly: polytechnic college, a college with mainly technical and scientific courses
manage: have enough money
student loan: money from government that students pay back when they start work
waiting on her at table: working as a waitress in the college halls

Caroline herself was not so sure. Academic excellence* was not always enough. You had to know the right people*, you had to be lucky, you had to network*. And where was the best place to begin a lifetime* of networking? Cambridge. A large percentage of the people who would be in key* jobs in a few years' time were currently studying at Cambridge. But they weren't all at Trinity; there were so many other colleges. How could she meet and, more importantly, impress them?

This was why Caroline needed the Cleopatra Club. The club was going to change her life, she thought. She sat at her desk now, writing the rules, and paused. She looked around the oak-panelled* room she shared with Sara for inspiration*.

Their room was in Neville's Court, a cloister-like* square overlooking passing tourists and students.

"Wow!" Caroline couldn't help herself, when she first walked through the great gateway* and into the arched courtyard*.

"Don't get too excited," cautioned* the third-year student who was showing her round*. "All this stone might be great in some Italian monastery*, but it's really damp and gets incredibly* slippery* in the winter."

academic excellence: getting very good grades at school or university
right people: people who can help you (get what you want)
network: meet and talk to people useful to one's career
lifetime: the whole of one's life
key: (here) very important
oak-panelled: walls covered in oak (a wood)
inspiration: new ideas and thoughts
cloister-like: like the squares with a covered surrounding corridor often found in cathedrals or monasteries
gateway: large open area for gate or door
courtyard: square area surrounded by a building
cautioned: warned
showing her around: taking her round the college, showing her where everything was
monastery: convent building where monks live
incredibly: very
slippery: hard to walk on

But Caroline had been excited, and she still was; she had simply learned to hide it.

"Why do we want a new club?" Sara had asked Caroline, when she first mentioned her idea.

"Why?" answered Caroline, gazing* out of the window. "Because most of the clubs are rubbish." Below, an elderly man was pushing a bicycle that looked as old as he did. He had a fluff* of white hair on top of a bald* head, which looked rather like a chick that has just emerged* from its egg. Caroline turned back to Sara, who was looking up names in an index.

"Do you know, there are about two hundred and fifty registered clubs and societies at the University? I looked it up. But most of them are so . . . well, nothing. They don't achieve anything."

"Are they meant to?" asked Sara, putting down the book and adding it to a pile on her desk.

"Some of them are," replied Caroline. "And some of them are great. The theatre clubs are fine if you want to act, and the sports clubs for sports people, and the Entrepreneurs'* Club for all those would-be* entrepreneurs. But a lot of them are just excuses* to get drunk."

"You can include the sports clubs on that list," agreed Sara, who had been amazed at the amount of beer the Trinity hockey team had drunk after a recent match. She was still a member of the club, even though she hadn't made* the team.

gazing: looking
fluff: (here) small amount of soft hair
bald: without hair
emerged: come out of
entrepreneurs: people who start up companies and take risks
would-be: who want to be; potential
excuses: false reasons for doing something
made: been selected for

"Yes. Too true," Caroline nodded. "I'm not interested in that. It's such a waste of time."

Sara laughed. Caroline was always complaining that there weren't enough hours in the day. She couldn't imagine her room-mate taking time out to get drunk. She'd never met anyone as focused* and motivated* as Caroline. She couldn't imagine feeling like that.

"I couldn't believe it when I first arrived," Caroline continued. "You walk into that huge sports hall and there are, like, hundreds of people shouting and playing music and leaping* about and trying to get you to join their clubs."

"Yes," agreed Sara. "I think I signed up to about fifty clubs. I just never went to their meetings."

Caroline laughed. "Yes, everyone does that, don't they? I found something called the Diplomacy Club and I thought it sounded great – a chance to meet people who were interested in languages and current affairs*..."

Sara laughed now. "Oh, Caroline! Diplomacy's a board game*."

"So I found out." Caroline pulled a face*.

focused: determined
motivated: with good reasons to do what she does
leaping: jumping
current affairs: political events and issues of the day
board game: game such as chess, played on a marked board
pulled a face: made an expression of disgust

"Did you go to a meeting?" Sara tried to imagine Caroline sitting round a table, playing a board game. She failed.

Caroline looked shocked. "Good heavens*, no. I looked them up on their website. Really silly. Like the Tiddlywinks* Club. What a waste of people's time. I can just about understand people playing chess. It's a good way to learn strategies*, but tiddlywinks. How sad is that*!"

"Yeah," Sara nodded. "You can just imagine the students who play, can't you? Earnest* scientists . . ."

". . . and social scientists . . ."

". . . and maths students . . ."

The girls laughed. It was a familiar game, being rude about students not lucky enough to read Humanities* like them. The division between science and the arts was as strong as ever. Each group looked down on the other, even though as members of the same college, they could often be sitting next to each other in hall for dinner.

Caroline had tried to explain the collegiate* system to her parents before she came up to the University.

"I don't understand," said her mother. You want to go to Cambridge, but you're applying to Trinity."

good heavens: expression of surprise
tiddlywinks: children's game where small plastic discs are flicked into a cup
strategies: ways of planning things to get the best results
how sad is that!: That's pathetic!
earnest: serious
Humanities: subjects such as arts, literature and history
collegiate: university system based on colleges

"Yes," explained Caroline. "Trinity is one of the Cambridge colleges. Cambridge is a collegiate university; every student is a member of a particular college. You live and eat and do most things within your own college. The colleges aren't just halls of residence*. They are also involved in teaching. They organise tutorials where you discuss your work with a professor or lecturer. It's all very one-to-one*. That's what makes Cambridge so different. And it means that within your college you mix with people studying all kinds of different subjects."

The reality was not quite the same. The science and arts students only got together to talk about films or sports or other joint* interests. The split* remained. But another fact of college life that Caroline had discovered was that it was hard to meet like-minded* people outside your own college and subject.

Caroline had joined the university newspaper and wrote regularly for *Varsity** and occasionally submitted* poems to its sibling* arts magazine. There she met all the current* university would-be media stars*. But she knew there must be other clever female students out there in the university who she wasn't meeting.

halls of residence: where students live and sleep
one-to-one: one student with one teacher
joint: shared
split: division
like-minded: people who thought like you
Varsity: Cambridge University newspaper
submitted: sent in
sibling: owned by the same publisher; sister magazine
current: at the present time
would-be media stars: who wanted a successful career in the media (newspapers, TV etc)

CAMBRIDGE
FOOTLIGHTS
The
Scarlet

A few days after Caroline had sat in Trinity Café and been inspired, she returned there with a group of female Varsity writers. She wanted to discuss the idea of the club with them. If they agreed, she knew it would be a success. Many of the same posters were still on the walls. Caroline pointed to the poster advertising the next Footlights evening.

"That's it," she said.

"What's it?" asked the film editor, Shabana, whose family came from Bombay, and who had an encyclopaedic* knowledge of British films.

"Footlights," continued Caroline, pointing to the poster. "It's the most successful Cambridge society there's ever been. Half the people at BBC once belonged to Footlights."

"And the other half were at Oxford," commented* the arts reviewer* wryly*.

"Exactly," said Caroline.

The students nodded. Cambridge Footlights was known all over the world. It was the home of Cambridge comedy. Each term the club put on a show with all the funniest and most successful actors and comedians.

"Everyone knows about Footlights," said Caroline. In some ways she thought it summed up* Cambridge University. It was where really talented* people could meet and work together. It was the perfect example of everything she'd always wanted. But it would never be the

encyclopaedic: very wide
commented: said
arts reviewer: someone who writes about arts events in a magazine or newspaper
wryly: showing amusement
summed up: represented
talented: people with natural ability

right club for her. She wasn't Emma Thompson nor John Cleese nor Stephen Fry, nor any of the other former Footlights heroes, who now ran* Britain's theatres, were television producers and had their own television comedy shows.

Caroline Kitson had many talents, but she could not act, and humour was not one of her attributes*. Indeed, some people said that Caroline had no sense of humour* at all.

"We need a new club because there are no clubs dedicated to helping women through university and in the real world afterwards," she said. "Nothing like the American sororities*. What we want ..." She paused. She had nearly said, 'I want', but had stopped herself in time. "What we want is a club that will do* for women, whatever they are studying, what Footlights has done for all the people who have wanted to go into comedy."

"A kind of sisterhood* for the successful," smiled Shabana. "Whatever they say, men still have ways of helping each other that exclude* women. It'd be good to try and reverse* that."

"Absolutely," said the political correspondent*, who came from Liverpool and found that many people at Cambridge treated her differently* because of her Liverpudlian* accent.

"And the club will attract the very best . . ." continued Caroline.

ran: controlled, managed
attributes: qualities
sense of humour: ability to appreciate jokes
sororities: female societies at American universities
do: achieve; get
sisterhood: a society of women; women helping each other
exclude: keep out
reverse: make the opposite happen
political correspondent: someone who writes about politics
treated her differently: behaved in a different way towards her than to other people
Liverpudlian: from Liverpool

"Yes." They all nodded.

"Sounds a bit élitist," grumbled* a student known for her political correctness*.

"And Footlights isn't?" asked Caroline

"Good point*," said Shabana. "You have to be good to get into that*. Their auditions* are really tough*. I know," she laughed, "because I didn't get in myself."

"Well, there you are*!" Caroline smiled. "Footlights is a precedent*. And we can apply for up to a thousand pounds from the Amalgamated* Clubs fund* to start the club up."

"So, how do we get members?" "So, what do we call it?" asked Shabana and the arts editor simultaneously*.

"The Cleopatra Club," said Caroline, amazed that she was selling them the idea so quickly.

"Why Cleo?" asked another journalist. "Wasn't she just all beauty and black eyeliner*?"

"That was Liz Taylor in the movie," said Shabana.

grumbled: complained
political correctness: the opinion that everyone should be treated in the same way
good point: what you've said is true
get into that: be allowed to join
auditions: acting tests to get a part in a play
tough: difficult
there you are: that proves what I said
precedent: something that has happened in the past that can be used as a model for the present
amalgamated: joined together
fund: sum of money for special purposes
simultaneously: at the same time
eyeliner: black line of make-up on the eyelid

"Quite*," added Caroline. "Cleopatra was a clever, shrewd* politician, who managed to get Julius Caesar to put her on the throne. She knew what she wanted and how she could get it."

A few of the students glanced at each other. To them Cleopatra sounded* remarkably* like Caroline. But the idea of the club appealed*.

"How do we get ourselves known?" asked the arts editor.

"Do it informally* at first. By invitation," suggested Caroline. "Then when we've got enough members to make a committee, we write a piece* in *Varsity*."

"Why don't we write an attack on the club in *Varsity*?" asked the political correspondent.

"What? Why?" asked Caroline.

"Because if someone writes a piece, you know, saying that it's not fair because it is élitist and that losers* can't get in…"

"…then those who aren't losers will be interested," finished Shabana.

"That's brilliant," said Caroline. "I'll get Sara to put her name to it."

"I am brilliant," smiled the correspondent. "That's why I want to be a member."

quite: that's right
shrewd: with good judgement
sounded: reminded them of
remarkably: notably
appealed: attracted them
informally: by talking to friends
piece: article
losers: people who are unsuccessful or thought to be so

"You will be a member. What about the Chair*?" asked Shabana.

"Caroline. Of course."

"Of course."

Caroline smiled.

The Club was an immediate success. It was mentioned in several Sunday newspapers, praised by *The Economist** and attacked by three left-wing commentators*. The chairwomen of several international organisations agreed to come and give talks to the Club. Caroline wrote a series of features* on glass ceilings* in different fields* and how they were beginning to be dismantled*. The head of the careers office* called her in* to thank her and offered her introductions to other senior* businesswomen who might be interested in the Club.

The Cleopatra Club was everything Caroline had hoped it would be.

The moment that the Cleopatra Club came into being*, Sara knew that she had to become a member, whatever it took*, whatever she had to do. But everyone thought she hated the club because of the article in *Varsity*. Caroline hadn't even told her about it until the article came out and did not seem to understand why her room-mate was so upset.

Chair: chairman/woman; head of a society or company
The Economist: weekly British business magazine
left-wing commentators: people working for the media with liberal and left-wing opinions
features: articles
glass ceilings: invisible barriers that prevent women getting the top jobs
fields: occupations; areas
dismantled: got rid of; removed
careers office: university department that advises students on jobs
called her in: invited her to the office
senior: of high rank
came into being: started
whatever it took: whatever was necessary

It all made it even harder for her to become a member, thought Sara, but she knew her father would be pleased if she joined. Though Caroline wasn't going to make it easy.

"Of course I'd love you to be a member, Sara. You just have to prove yourself*. Like anyone else who wants to join," said Caroline. Then she told Sara just what that meant.

"An initiation ceremony*. What do you mean?" the political correspondent asked at one of the club's first committee meetings, when Caroline suggested the idea. "Do you mean something like they have in those American colleges . . . what do they call it?"

"Hazing," someone replied.

"Yes. Hazing," continued the correspondent. "Awful! Like the kind of rituals* that you have to go through to join a gang*. People die doing those kinds of things, Caroline."

"We don't want anything like that," said June, an early member of the Club, who everyone knew had a brilliant future ahead of her in banking*. "From what I've read they mostly involve drinking huge amounts of alcohol. I wouldn't want anything to do with that kind of thing," she added. "It's degrading*, dangerous and nothing to do with the aims of the Club."

"Quite," said Caroline, feeling that she was losing control of the meeting. "I don't know who mentioned hazing in the first place. No. I

prove yourself: show you are good enough to join
initiation ceremony: test to see if people are good enough to join
rituals: set of actions often performed in a fixed order
gang: group of people, often criminal
banking: working for a bank
degrading: treating people without respect

think we should get prospective* members to invent their own scenarios*. They simply have to come and tell us what they've done and why."

"A presentation*?" said June, thoughtfully.

"Yes," said Caroline. "And we can judge their presentation skills at the same time."

The committee nodded.

"But how will they know what to do?" asked another committee member.

"We just tell them that they need to stretch themselves*, " said Caroline "They have to do something brave…whatever they feel is appropriate*."

"That's brilliant, Caro," said June. The Committee agreed and the initiation ceremonies began.

Sara's heart fell at the news. What could she do that was brave or clever enough to amaze Caroline? she wondered. She became even more determined to join the Club. She just had to find a way of impressing* the committee.

Caroline herself was quite impressed at the lengths students went to* in order to join the club. There was a tiny red-haired girl studying medicine at Clare College who climbed a 30-foot fir tree and then took photographs of the College from the top. She displayed* the

prospective: people who want to join
scenarios: plans of action
presentation: short talk to present information
stretch themselves: make full use of their talents
appropriate: suitable; acceptable,
impressing: making them admire her
lengths students went to: the amount of effort students made
displayed: showed

photographs at her presentation, and not one of them was blurred or out of focus*. Despite her position, she had held her hand perfectly steady.

"Why did you chose to do this?" asked June

"Because I suffer from vertigo*," said the girl. "It was the hardest thing I could think of."

Caroline smiled at her. "And if we asked you to do it again?"

"I'd say that there is no virtue* in repetition*. Find me a new tree."

Caroline laughed. She looked round the table. They all nodded. "Welcome to the Cleopatra Club," she said.

The next applicant* arrived with an egg. She handed it to Caroline. The egg was small and had a tiny feather still stuck to it.

"I'm scared of birds," said the applicant, still shivering* from the encounter*. "But I found a farm where they have free-range chickens* and I lifted the hen to get the egg."

Caroline took the egg from the girl and broke it into a glass.

"Drink it," she ordered.

The girl smiled. She opened her bag and took out a bottle of hot

blurred/out of focus: when the image in a photograph is unclear
vertigo: fear of heights
virtue: positive quality
repetition: doing the same thing again
applicant: someone who wants to join something
shivering: shaking (with shock or fear)
encounter: what she had met
free-range chickens: chickens that live outside and run about freely

Worcestershire Sauce and a salt and pepper grinder*. She added the sauce and salt and pepper to the egg and stirred it up without breaking the yolk*. Then she swallowed it in one gulp*.

"I had a feeling you'd ask me to do that," she said staring at Caroline. "You have quite a reputation*."

Caroline laughed. "I like people who think ahead," she replied. The Club gained* another member.

One student planted flowers during the night on the Master's lawn*. They formed* the answer to a complicated mathematical equation*. Another student showed the committee her share portfolio*. She had taken out a student loan and invested* all of it in high-risk shares*, doubling her money in a week. She now had a serious* portfolio. She and June immediately became friends.

Sara was horrified* when Caroline told her.

"What if she'd lost all her money? She wouldn't have had anything to live on."

Caroline shrugged*. "If you're going to take a risk, you have to be

grinder: that crushes salt and pepper into a fine powder
yolk: yellow centre of an egg
gulp: swallow
quite a reputation: people say a lot of things about you
gained: got
Master's lawn: the Master or Mistress is the head of a Cambridge college. Students are not allowed to walk in their gardens or on their lawns (grass) without permission.
formed: made the shape of
equation: a statement showing that two amounts are equal; formula
share portfolio: list of shares (money put into companies) that someone owns and can buy and sell
invested: put
high-risk shares: shares that can suddenly go up or down in value
serious: worth a lot of money
horrified: shocked
shrugged: moved her shoulders up and down to show she didn't care

prepared to lose as well as win."

"Would you do it with your scholarship fund?" asked Sara.

"Of course not," said Caroline sharply*. "It's not my kind of thing*. I'm not a gambler*." She turned to Sara. "I see your name is down* for next month's Cleopatra presentations. What are you going to do?"

"I can't tell you that," said Sara, but in fact she still had not decided what she was going to do. It would probably be something to do with swimming, as she was scared of water. It went back to when she was five and her brother had thrown her into the deep end of a swimming pool.

Sara walked along the River Cam looking for inspiration. The sun was setting* behind a line of scrubby* bushes, and ducks and moorhens* scurried* along the surface of the water like weekend drivers heading* home. If only she could do something dramatic* like work out the solution to the Mathematical Bridge*, which, when it was first built, didn't need rivets* to hold it together. Then she had an idea.

The next day she borrowed some canvas* from the theatre club and then a large battery from the science labs. She worked secretly. She didn't want Caroline to find out what she was doing. Then, early the following morning, Sara went down to the river and took one of the canoes* that were tied up by Magdalene Bridge. She stepped gingerly*

sharply: angrily
my kind of thing: what I do
gambler: someone who bets money on things
is down: is on a list
setting: going down
scrubby: small; unimportant
moorhens: small black water birds
scurried: moved quickly
heading: going
dramatic: (here) exciting and unusual
Mathematical Bridge: bridge at Queens' College, Cambridge
rivets: pieces of metal that hold things together
canvas: material (used for painting and making sails)
canoes: small narrow boats without engines
gingerly: carefully

into the canoe and started to paddle* down river. The current was faster than she had expected and soon she was heading towards the deep water around Fen Ditton. Just beyond there was an island with one tree on it. It was here that she was going to land and erect* her banner*, which, as soon as it got dark, would spell out the words "Cleopatra Club" in small lights.

There wasn't a proper place to land the canoe on the island, however, and as she tried to jump onto solid ground, her foot slipped and she fell back into the river. The current immediately pulled her back into its fast-moving flow* and the weeds* clutched at her feet, pulling her under. Sara struggled, but she was not strong enough. The weeds pulled her under the water and held her there.

From Camcorder, the Cambridge gossip column* of *Varsity*:

News has reached this office of the collapse of that fearsome* female society, the Cleopatra Club. After the tragic* death of Sara Hand, who is still much missed* in Trinity circles*, this can't be a surprise to anyone. And speaking of the much missed . . . has anyone seen Caroline Kitson this term, or has the former club leader disappeared, too?*

paddle: move using a paddle (piece of wood used to move a canoe)
erect: put up
banner: long strip of material with writing
flow: current
weeds: plants growing wild
gossip column: where information is written about people's lives and habits
collapse: ending
fearsome: frightening
tragic: extremely sad
missed: her loss is felt
Trinity circles: in the college

After Reading

Response

Ⓐ How did you think the story was going to end? Were you shocked by the ending when you read it?

Ⓑ What do you think of Caroline? Did your feelings towards her change as you read the story?

Ⓒ Would you like to be a student at Cambridge University? Why/Why not?

Comprehension

Ⓐ Read the first three rules of the Cleopatra Club and decide whether the following statements are True or False.

	True	False
All members of the club will be women.	☐	☐
Any Cambridge University student can join the club.	☐	☐
To become a member of the club you have to pay the committee.	☐	☐
Only clever students can join the club.	☐	☐
Students can complain to the committee if they are not chosen.	☐	☐

After Reading

Ⓑ Complete the sentences with the correct names.

.... founded Trinity College in 1546.
.... was a favourite of Queen Elizabeth I.
.... was India's first prime minister.
.... was a Nobel prize-winner.
.... kept a bear in his room.
.... discovered the law of gravity.

• Bertrand Russell • Henry VIII • Nehru
• Sir Isaac Newton • Byron • The Earl of Essex

Ⓒ "Caroline felt like a cuckoo in an uncomfortably small nest." Explain why Caroline felt like this, giving examples from the text.

Ⓓ Give three reasons why Caroline was excited by Cambridge.

Ⓔ Which of the following phrases are about Sara (S), which are about her brother (B) and which are about her father (F)?

	S	B	F
won a place to study history	☐	☐	☐
was a well-known historian	☐	☐	☐
had studied at Trinity many years before	☐	☐	☐
had studied at Oxford	☐	☐	☐
thought the university was élitist	☐	☐	☐
was a rugby player	☐	☐	☐
was a brilliant student	☐	☐	☐
tried to get into the university hockey team	☐	☐	☐
secretly hated Cambridge	☐	☐	☐

After Reading

Ⓕ Complete the following sentences.

Sara wanted to be Caroline's friend because ....
Boys spent evenings with Sara because.................................
Sara felt uncomfortable because...
Caroline felt insecure because..
Caroline needed the Cleopatra Club because.........................

Ⓖ Which of the following clubs and societies did Sara or Caroline like and which did they not like?

	Liked	Didn't like
Theatre clubs	☐	☐
Sports clubs	☐	☐
The Entrepreneur Club	☐	☐
The Diplomacy Club	☐	☐
The Tiddlywinks Club	☐	☐
Footlights	☐	☐

Ⓗ Why did the students think that Cleopatra sounded like Caroline?

Ⓘ Which of the following are reasons for joining the Cleopatra Club?

- networking ☐
- having parties ☐
- drinking a lot of alcohol ☐
- producing a newspaper ☐
- getting information from successful businesswomen ☐
- producing plays and comedy shows ☐
- meeting the brightest students in Cambridge ☐

Ⓙ Using the following phrases and, without looking back at the text, describe what the applicants did in order to join the club.

- suffered from vertigo - climbed a 30-foot fir tree - took photographs - no blurry images
- scared of birds – lifted hen – took egg – had sauce in handbag – swallowed egg
- planted flowers – Master's lawn – answer to equation
- took out loan – bought high-risk shares – doubled money

Ⓚ What was Sara trying to do before she had her tragic accident?

Plot and Setting

Ⓐ There are several flashbacks in the story. Put the following events in the order in which they actually happened.

Caroline writes the Club rules.	
Caroline has the idea for the Club.	
Caroline has rows with her mother at home.	
Caroline arrives in Cambridge.	
Caroline talks to Sara about the Club.	
Caroline describes Cambridge to her parents.	
Caroline has a meeting with other *Varsity* writers.	
The first applicants do their presentations.	
Sara tries to join the club.	
The club collapses.	

After Reading

Ⓑ Read the following sentences. Which do you think is the most important to the development of the plot? Explain the reasons for your choice.

- The idea of the Cleopatra Club had come to Caroline several weeks ago. ☐
- At seventeen, Caroline won a scholarship to go to Trinity College at Cambridge. ☐
- "I'll get Sara to put her name to it." ☐
- "... You have to be prepared to lose as well as win." ☐

Ⓒ What do you think happened to Caroline at the end of the story?

Ⓓ What impression does the author give of Trinity College and Cambridge? Tick the words which you think match her description.

- traditional ☐
- modern ☐
- ancient ☐
- élitist ☐
- cheap ☐
- historical ☐
- enclosed ☐
- ugly ☐
- fashionable ☐
- lively ☐

Ⓔ How does the author contrast Cambridge with the place where Caroline grew up?

After Reading

Theme

Ⓐ The central theme of this story is the desire people have to belong to a group. Which of the two main characters do you think wants to belong more, Caroline or Sara? Give reasons for your choice.

Ⓑ The story is also about being élitist. What are your feelings about élitism? Have your feelings changed as a result of reading this story?

Narration and Style

Ⓐ From whose point of view is the story told? Does the point of view change? Give examples.

Ⓑ How does the author characterise Caroline's mother? How does this differ from the other characterisations in the story?

Ⓒ The author uses a number of flashbacks. Look carefully at the points in the story where these occur. What effect do they have on your understanding of 'present' events?

Character

Ⓐ Write a description of Caroline as seen by Sara.

Ⓑ Write a description of Sara as seen by Caroline.

Ⓒ Apart from Caroline and Sara, the remaining characters in the story could be described as 'flat'. But Caroline and Sara are the opposite: they are 'rounded' characters; we know more about them.
How does the author achieve this?

After Reading

Vocabulary work

Ⓐ Match the following words with their definitions

eligibility	occasions when a group gets together
committee	people who belong to a club
members	unpleasant ritual for people joining a club
rules	someone who wants to join a club
hazing	group of people who organise something
applicant	another name for a club
meetings	what you must or must not do
society	qualification to join a club

Ⓑ Say which of the following words you think is Positive or Negative.

	Positive	Negative
assured	☐	☐
attractive	☐	☐
brave	☐	☐
brilliant	☐	☐
dangerous	☐	☐
degrading	☐	☐
disgusting	☐	☐
earnest	☐	☐
intimidating	☐	☐
motivated	☐	☐
ruthless	☐	☐
unassuming	☐	☐

After Reading

Ask the Author

Read all the author's questions and answers. Then do the following exercises.

Ⓐ Read the following statements and choose True or False.

	True	False
The Cleopatra Club is based on a Cambridge society called "Women of Trinity".	☐	☐
"Women of Trinity" does not allow men to attend events.	☐	☐
New laws in England may mean the end of men-only clubs.	☐	☐
Currently women cannot drink in golf club bars even though they can play golf.	☐	☐

Ⓑ Match the sentence and phrase openings with the correct endings.

The story is fictional but . . .	. . . historically accurate.
What the characters say about Footlights club is . . .	. . . because I ran a film festival.
I lived in Cambridge . . .	. . . I spent quite a lot of time there.
Though I wasn't a student at Cambridge . . .	. . . the setting is factual.
The information about Trinity College is . . .	. . . quite authentic.
I got to know the city . . .	. . . for ten years.

After Reading

Ⓒ Which of the following support the idea that Cambridge University is élitist?

- The University does everything it can to be open to everyone. ☐
- Entry is based on merit. ☐
- You have to get very good grades in your exams. ☐
- Oxford and Cambridge are different from other universities in England. ☐
- When you get to Cambridge there is this sense you are in a very special place. ☐
- Students from Cambridge's other university sometimes work for Cambridge students. ☐

Ⓓ Choose the correct answers

1. Men use clubs to:
a) get top jobs.
b) support each other.
c) meet the Prime Minister.

2. The 'glass ceiling'
a) is quickly disappearing.
b) is an invisible barrier to promotion.
c) is fashionable in many new homes.

3. The author
a) fought for her country.
b) fought for equal rights.
c) wanted to be Prime Minister.

4. The author feels that hazing
a) is just like bullying.
b) should be controlled.
c) gets rid of weaker club members.

After Reading

Follow-up

Speaking

Work in two groups. One group plays the role of committee members for a club and the other group are applicants wanting to join the club. Applicants give reasons for wanting to join and committee members give reasons for allowing or not allowing them to join.

Writing

Write an article for *Varsity* on the history of the Cleopatra Club. You can use the information in the story and also invent additional information.

Or

Write a letter from Caroline to Sara's family explaining what happened.

Class activity

Invent a club. Say what the purpose of the club will be and why you want it. Then make up some of the club rules.

Notes

Notes